X-MEN

AND THE

BOOK OF REVELATION

X-Men and the Book of Revelation

Manning, Paul

X-MEN and the Book of Revelation / Paul Manning

293 p. 23cm × 15cm (9in × 6 in.)
ISBN 978-0-9975266-0-8

1. Bible. N.T. Revelation-Commentaries. 2. Superheroes. 3. End-Times, Apocalyptic II. Title.

Printed in the United States of America.

Fourth Edition

4 5 6 7 8 9 10 11 12 / 22 21 20 19 18

X-MEN

AND THE

BOOK OF
REVELATION

REVEALING THE TRUTH ABOUT GOD'S APOCALYPSE

WITH UNCANNY INSIGHTS FROM THE X-MEN

PAUL MANNING

Contents

Introduction

The spark that ignited my idea of writing of this verse-by-verse analysis of the Bible's last book (Revelation) – accompanied by uncanny insights from various characters in the X-Men universe – came about during the summer of 2014. It was then that I learned of the global excitement generated by the announcement of the movie *X-Men: Apocalypse* (premiered and released globally in May 2016). Featuring fictional super-powered mutants (good and not-so-good) uniting to battle against an evil super-powered mutant who has assumed the name of Apocalypse, the announcement of this movie created a frenzy of eager anticipation among millions who enjoy the genre of superhero fiction.

Since its release, *X-Men: Apocalypse* has entertained millions of people from nations around the world and grossed over half of a billion dollars. While it received mixed reviews, this book is not meant to critique the movie's quality or even storyline. Rather, the purpose of this book is to shed light on what the Bible really has to say about end-of-the-world topics such as the apocalypse, the four horsemen of the apocalypse, disastrous conditions, and the fate of the world.

Beyond superhero, zombie, and action fiction that are often based on world-ending story lines, non-fiction news around the world report on real issues each day that threaten to usher in doomsday scenarios. Undoubtedly, in the minds of many people are swirling real questions pertaining to life's meaning, Bible prophecy and the truth of the book of Revelation.

As I began writing this book in the fall of 2015, news headlines around the world were filled with conflicts and wars. Specifically, there were about 50 known armed conflicts occurring at that time in various nations (see the following link for details: http:// en.wikipedia.org/wiki/List_of_ongoing_armed_conflicts).

In addition to the current scenario of wars and rumors of wars, there is great economic instability, famine, disease outbreaks, cyber-threats, and other emerging crises that cause hearts and minds to be perplexed and filled with anxiety. Many people wonder if the threat of apocalyptic events will become a reality in our lifetime.

Fear of natural disasters, man-made weapons of mass-destruction, along with other threats that could wipe out tens of thousands, or even millions, have people in a state of concern about their physical well-being and hopes for the future. Also troubling hearts all around the world are threats of financial ruin carried out by evil people – whether by way of cyber-attacks or other diabolical actions – which could send nations into chaos overnight. Thinking about such things leave people restless and in constant turmoil.

In light of this reality, the million-dollar question is this: Does it really matter what *you* believe about issues pertaining to "end-time" events – especially if your life currently seems unaffected by the global turmoil you only read and hear about in the news? It is not my intent to personally answer this question for you. But my purpose in writing this book is to explain what the Bible really has to say about the real upcoming apocalypse, offering an easy-to-understand and factual explanation of the last days and the future world to come.

The popularity of a movie such as *X-Men: Apocalypse* – which has a world-ending theme that includes disasters (both natural and man-/mutant-made), global fear, and mass casualties – reveals an ironic dichotomy in the eagerness of fans of this genre. On one hand, millions of them eagerly wanted to see the movie's fictional apocalyptic character and experience the cinematic thrill of him wreaking havoc on the world. Conversely, those same moviegoers are not likely to ever want to personally experience a true apocalyptic scenario – regardless of how many heroes show up to help them.

In consideration of this contradiction, the following chapters will examine God's true apocalyptic literature – coupled with statements and unique insights from super-powered fictional mutants – with the goals of enlightening inquiring minds with biblical truth about the apocalypse and liberating worried hearts from end-of-the-world myths, lies, and confusion.

Like so many people alive today, I did not grow up particularly interested in spiritual things. My lack of interest, however, was not due to an inherent dislike of God or an immoral lifestyle. No, my lack of interest was because no one and/or nothing had ever challenged me to pause from the trivial pursuits of life and learn what God has actually told us about life's meaning, end-of-the-world issues, and what's after death.

That changed when I was nineteen years old. Once I took steps to learn for myself what the Bible had to say about life and what's after death, my opinions, beliefs, hopes, decisions, and eternal destiny were radically altered. The express purpose of this writing is that readers may have the opportunity to personally examine what God has to say in the book of Revelation and then decide how they will prepare for the coming apocalypse.

Understanding the book of Revelation doesn't require a PhD or other letters behind a person's name, but only the sincere desire to know what God has to say about life, both temporal and eternal, as well as a desire to grow in your devotion to Him. The Bible, including the book of Revelation, is not meant to be mysterious and unknowable. On the contrary, God has given us this dynamic, action-packed, and life-changing book for the purpose of enlightening us concerning His truths and purposes.

Since 1987, I have been studying and teaching the Bible to a wide array of people, including church groups, college athletes, inner-city and suburban youth, politicians, entertainers, corporate executives, and neighbors. In 1992 I founded a high-performance athletic and biblical discipleship academy for youth that has, since then, impacted thousands of kids, young adults, and families in its unique 150,000 square foot training center.

I must admit I've found this book especially fun to write because it connects my passions for helping people grow intellectually, emotionally, and spiritually with one of my childhood passions – superhero comic books. I began reading superhero comics at the age of six. By the age of eight, having voraciously read many superhero-based books, I decided that I wanted to become a superhero. Don't laugh; I was serious about this! At age eleven, I began taking martial arts lessons (including weapons) and gymnastics. Long before STEM (science, technology, engineering, and math) was a popular term, I was reading about it in comics and began thinking about how I would utilize various technologies to achieve my goal.

Around the age nine or ten, having learned about technologies such as Iron Man's suit of armor and repulsor rays, Captain America's shield, and Spider-Man's web-shooters (utilizing nanotechnology), I began reading about titanium alloys, laser technology, jet propulsion, and hydraulics in encyclopedias (I told you that I was serious). After collecting over five hundred comics and doing research and training over the next few years, I finally realized that I would not become a superhero. However, the comics and my research led me to later obtain a degree in electrical engineering from Virginia Tech. Long story made short, my passions and studies in the areas of comics, martial arts, engineering, and the Bible have all culminated in the writing this book with the hope that its contents will to captivate, motivate, and illuminate the minds, hearts, and souls of readers.

Within the following chapters, readers will learn the truth about real super-powered beings who actually exist in the universe and will one day enter our dimension (the earthly realm) to be seen and heard by the masses. These beings will engage in both action and communication that will bring to light the secret war in the heavens that has been hidden from our world's view. These are beings that fly, travel in different dimensions, have super strength, control the elements, and fight to protect the future of mankind. By the end of our study, it will become apparent that the powers of the fictional superheroes read about in comic books and seen in movies are actually modeled after some of the heavenly beings that are revealed in the last book of the Bible.

So, if you've ever wanted to know what the truth is regarding how the world will one day experience a climactic battle that involves humans, super-powered agents of good, beasts, storms, demonic beings, and the all-powerful One who is referred to as the Alpha and Omega (Greek for the First and the Last), then you've come to the right place. It is my sincere hope that this book will not be a source of information by which you can increase your apocalyptic and biblical knowledge, but that your mind would be captivated, your heart convicted, and your life transformed as you consider the marvel of God's revealed plans.

Chapter 1

What (or Who) Is the Apocalypse – Really?

MUTANT INSIGHT

Apocalypse: "I am Apocalypse. Look upon the future—and tremble."

[X-Men The Animated Series: Come the Apocalypse]

The two important words in the quote above from Apocalypse are "future" and "tremble". This super-being is giving the "revelation" that he has come, after thousands of years of planning, to disrupt the natural cycle of the ebb and flow of life by destroying weak people – both humans and mutants. His purpose for doing this is to recreate the earth's population with a new master race. This new breed of more dominant mutants will exist to serve him as their master and lord. Apocalypse's declaration above indicates that what he plans to do will cause everyone who opposes him to tremble in their boots, be overwhelmed with fear, and flee from his presence with the knowledge that their doom is eminent.

Great fiction for sure! However, in the following chapters, we will turn our attention to the last book of the Bible to learn the truth about the God's apocalypse and His plans regarding mankind and the future.

Beyond Thunderdome

In 1985, Tina Turner's hit song, "We Don't Need Another Hero (Thunderdome)" hit the airwaves and became one of her biggest worldwide hits. It was the theme song to the film *Mad Max Beyond Thunderdome* starring Mel Gibson. The lyrics of this song were written from the perspective of oppressed people whose quality of living has declined to a horrible state, causing them to live as nomads struggling to survive in their post-apocalyptic world. When Max shows up, they don't want to get their hopes up (again) in another supposed "hero" who may or may not be able to save them. Why are these people in the movie so fearful, doubtful, and hardened? Because in their hearts, minds, and life experiences they lack the following five core needs that one must have in order to live with hope, peace, and purpose:

- **Wonder** – the sense of admiration, excitement, or awe

- **Truth** – the pillar of trust

- **Love** – the greatest longing of all people

- **Security** – the desire for safety and peace

- **Hope** – the expectation of positive outcomes/future

In contrast, when one thinks of the word apocalypse, there are five quality-of-life destroyers that sweep into people's lives, subduing if not killing, the five core needs listed above, bringing despair and bondage:

- **Poverty**

- **Loss of love**

- **No sense of purpose**

- **Lack of security**

- **Illness / Death**

The meaning of the word apocalypse is commonly defined as:

> **a-poc-a-lypse,** *noun* – 1. The complete final de-
> struction of the world, especially as described in
> the biblical book of Revelation; 2. An event involv-
> ing destruction or damage on an awesome or cata-
> strophic scale.

The definitions above resonate with most of us, conjuring
up images we've seen in fictitious, end-of-the-world movies,
television shows, and video games – images of destroyed cities,
wastelands that have emerged from global nuclear war, and a
human population in decline and chaos.

With regard to Marvel's fictitious mutant villain named
Apocalypse, Bob Harras, who was editor-in-chief of Marvel
Comics from 1995 to 2000, said of this comic book character:

> He looked fantastic. Also, the name is dynamic. It
> tells you right off this character means trouble.
> And he came with a clear-cut agenda: 'survival of
> the fittest.' He didn't care if you were a mutant—if
> you were weak, you would be destroyed. He was
> merciless, but his philosophy was easy to grasp and
> it fit in with the harder edge of evolution which is
> part and parcel of the mutant story. Isn't that what
> humans fear about mutants? That they are the next
> step? Now, we had given mutants something new to
> fear: a character who would judge them on their ge-
> netic worthiness. [...] To his own mind he wasn't evil
> (despite his leadership of the Alliance of Evil, which
> I think we dropped pretty soon after Apocalypse's

introduction); he believed he was doing the right thing. He was ensuring evolution. To me, he was the perfect next step in the mutant story.[1]

Now we know the creative thought that went into the development of the fictional X-Men adversary, Apocalypse. While the definition of the word apocalypse is defined the same way in both the news and entertainment media, did you know that the Bible's definition is not quite the same? Let's now dive into the last book of the Bible, the Revelation of Jesus Christ, and discover what the apocalypse is really about. Neither hesitate nor be afraid to read this prophetic book given to us by God. The cosmic enemy of your soul, Satan (aka the devil), wants to distract and intimidate you with wrong information or ideas so that you won't read it and learn the truth. However, this is what God himself says to all who would read the book of Revelation: "Blessed is the one who reads the words of this prophecy, and blessed are those who hear it and take to heart what is written in it, because the time is near." [Revelation 1:3] The end goal? "Then you will know the truth, and the truth will set you free." [John 8:32]

MUTANT INSIGHT

Apocalypse: "You're all my children. And you're lost because you follow blind leaders. These false gods, systems of the weak, they've ruined my world – no more!"
Psylokce: "What do you want?"
Apocalypse: "I want you...to feel the full reach of your powers. You've only had a taste of your true strength – unlike others who seek to control you [referring to Caliban], I want to set you free."

[X-Men: Apocalypse]

10

As seen in the movie *X-Men: Apocalypse*, Apocalypse is awakened after 5,583 years of a pseudo-burial and resumes his quest to rule the world. One of his strategies in doing so is to recruit four powerful mutants who he can mind-control to be his henchmen. These four mutants are referred to as his "four horsemen of Apocalypse" – and use their great powers to help him conquer weak humans and mutants.

In the exchange above, Apocalypse tells Psylocke (as well as Storm and Caliban) – a powerful mutant possessing telepathic and telekinetic powers – that she has been following blind leaders who have kept her in bondage, preventing her from reaching her full potential in life. He promises to give her freedom and purpose as she submits to his leadership. In actuality, Apocalypse has no desire to set her or others free. He is a liar, manipulator, and focused not on the well-being of others but, rather, only on his own exaltation as world leader and would-be-god.

As you continue to read this book, you will learn more about what the Bible says about God's desire to rescue people from the shackles of the devil – that powerful fallen angel from whom all fictitious evil characters such as Apocalypse are derived. About Satan, I Corinthians 4:4 says:

> The god of this age has blinded the minds of unbelievers, so that they cannot see the light of the gospel that displays the glory of Christ, who is the image of God.

Jesus said the following to a group who were vehemently opposing him:

> You belong to your father, the devil, and you want
> to carry out your father's desires. He was a murder-
> er from the beginning, not holding to the truth, for
> there is no truth in him. When he lies, he speaks his
> native language, for he is a liar and the father of lies.
> [John 8:44]

Contrasting the difference between the devil's agenda and his own, Jesus said to those following him,

> The thief [Satan] comes only to steal and kill and de-
> stroy; I have come that they may have life, and have
> it to the full. [John 10:1]

Chapter 2

The Future Unveiled

Revelation 1:1-8

MUTANT INSIGHT

Professor X: "They haven't learned how to live at ease with their mutant powers, so they are frustrated. Some lash out, while some have turned inward, letting their bitterness consume them. But they all feel dissatisfied with themselves – and alone."

[X-Men The Animated Series: Come the Apocalypse]

Professor Charles Xavier, also known as Professor X, is the fictional Marvel character who founded and leads the X-Men. He is a powerful telepath who not only can read people's minds, but can also talk to them mind-to-mind without audible speech. He also has the power to override people's will and make them do what he wants – though he uses this power very rarely and only for good, righteous, and noble deeds. He has taken hundreds of mutants into his academy, not only to teach them how to use their mutant powers, but more importantly, to care for them and provide for them a place of love, trust, and acceptance.

The truth of Xavier's statement above is relevant not only to fictitious comic book characters who struggle to find meaning in life, but also to everyday people such as you and me.

While humans don't have mutant powers, many are living lives of anxiety and frustration. These debilitating thoughts come from feelings of inferiority and a belief that they don't measure up to the standards of others. If not careful, these downward-spiraling thoughts can lead people into pits of seclusion from others and/ or bouts of rage when struggling to communicate with others – fearful that they may see us for who we are.

If you are dissatisfied with living a life of fear, bitterness, and isolation, then continue reading this book. In it are truths of God that will be unveiled to you – truths that are sometimes quietly hinted and at other times spoken overtly by comic heroes. These truths not only offer hope for your current daily life, but also give an assurance of peace and protection for the future – when the world will indeed experience literal cataclysmic, end-of-the-world scenarios often presented in apocalyptic books, movies, and television shows. You are not alone. God loves you. Like Professor X, He desires to love, teach, and care for you as his disciple. Trust him.

Hear It, Read It...Guaranteed Blessing!

Revelation 1:1-3

> [1] *The revelation of Jesus Christ, which God gave him to show his servants what must soon take place. He made it known by sending his angel to his servant John,* [2] *who testifies to everything he saw—that is, the word of God and the testimony of Jesus Christ.* [3] *Blessed is the one who reads the words of this prophecy, and blessed are those who hear it and take to heart what is written in it, because the time is near.*

* **Revelation 1:1** → The first sentence of this letter actually reveals what Revelation – the last book in the Bible – is all about:

God's unveiling of what will occur in heaven and on earth during the last days. This prophetic revealing of characters, events, timeframes, and Jesus' climatic second coming to earth was first given to Jesus (God the Son) from God the Father and then revealed to John, one of Jesus' twelve disciples.

It is important to note that the last book of the Bible, like the rest of the New Testament, was originally written in Greek and is spelled (in Greek) ἀποκάλυψις. When transliterated to English (which means writing the word using English alphabets instead of the Greek letters), this word is **apokalupsis**. The English spelling of the word is **apocalypse**. The biblical definition for this word is:

> **apocalypse**, *noun* – 1. An unveiling or uncovering;
> 2. A disclosure of truth; 3. A revealing.

Thus, the word "revelation" is where the Bible's Book of the Revelation of Jesus Christ gets its name. Now that we have the proper biblical definition of this word, we see that the word does not pertain, necessarily, to anything evil, fearful, or destructive. In the case of the prophetic last book of the Bible, the word apocalypse pertains to the revealing of truth that God wants to communicate to us – a truth that had not been previously revealed or known to mankind. Specifically, the truth being revealed in this book is the imminent second coming of the Lord Jesus Christ to reclaim his earth and establish his never-ending kingdom of righteousness. Reading and studying the Apocalypse (the Revelation) of Jesus Christ will do the following:

> Enlighten your mind and cause you to marvel at the
> Lord Jesus Christ like never before.
>
> Crush false beliefs perpetrated by Satan and his fol-
> lowers over the centuries.

Challenge you to decide how you will position your-self for eternity.

Touched by an Angelic Truth

The second sentence of Revelation 1:1 refers to an angel. The word "angel" means messenger. God has used angels from heaven in the past to provide specific messages from himself to various people, including Lot [Genesis 19:1-22], Daniel [Daniel 9:21; 10:4-21], and Mary [Luke 1:26-28]. In the comic book world, the X-Men character named Angel looks like an ordinary man except for his large white wings.

The biblical truth, however, is that real angels don't have wings. Some other beings have them (this will be discussed later), but angels do not. Also, while having the form of man, angels are distinctively different in their DNA from human beings. Throughout the Bible, their appearances vary in intensity when they are in the presence of humans, ranging from low-key forms that can't be differentiated from humans to their full-fledged appearances that radiate with heavenly splendor (gleaming like lightning) and super-power.

Daniel was a man whom God used to prophesy many things during the reigns of both Babylonian and Medo-Persian kings. He lived from approximately 604 B.C. through 534 B.C. He was an advisor to world leaders such as Nebuchadnezzar (Babylon), Darius (Persia), and Cyrus the Great (Persia). Check out what he saw and heard regarding the splendor and power of angels, as recorded in the Bible [Daniel 10:5-12]:

> I looked up and there before me was a man dressed
> in linen, with a belt of fine gold from Uphaz around
> his waist. His body was like topaz, his face like light-
> ning, his eyes like flaming torches, his arms and

legs like the gleam of burnished bronze, and his voice like the sound of a multitude. I, Daniel, was the only one who saw the vision; those who were with me did not see it, but such terror overwhelmed them that they fled and hid themselves. So I was left alone, gazing at this great vision; I had no strength left, my face turned deathly pale and I was helpless. Then I heard him speaking, and as I listened to him, I fell into a deep sleep, my face to the ground. A hand touched me and set me trembling on my hands and knees. He said, "Daniel, you who are highly esteemed, consider carefully the words I am about to speak to you, and stand up, for I have now been sent to you." And when he said this to me, I stood up trembling. Then he continued, "Do not be afraid, Daniel. Since the first day that you set your mind to gain understanding and to humble yourself before your God, your words were heard, and I have come in response to them.

Wow!! Angels like this are the true guardians of the galaxy.

* **Revelation 1:2** → John was called by Jesus to be one of his first disciples (eager and disciplined follower) and later appointed by Jesus to be one of his twelve apostles. John was used as God's instrument to write the Gospel of John (fourth book in the New Testament) as well as 1st, 2nd, and 3rd John (three short letters near the end of the New Testament). John was also used by God to write down the words of the Revelation, testifying to everything he saw and heard as Jesus unveiled end-time truths to him.

* **Revelation 1:3** → It is HIGHLY IMPORTANT to read, contemplate, and retain the words of this verse. Many today, are confused – even fearful – when reading this letter/book. That is exactly what Satan desires. The devil always uses deception

to distort people's understanding of God's Word (people who don't actually read and study it). The fact is, this verse informs us explicitly that whoever reads and/or hears the words of this prophetic book and takes it to heart WILL BE BLESSED – both in this life (temporal) and the one to come (eternal).

MUTANT INSIGHT

Wolverine: "Professor, Magneto's a lost cause. Why waste time on him?"

Professor X: "There were a dozen times when Erik could have handed us over to Apocalypse in exchange for his child, but he didn't – and that proves that there is hope for even the hardest of hearts."

[X-Men Legends II Rise of Apocalypse]

This exchange between Wolverine and Professor X is about Magneto (Erik is his first name), an incredibly powerful mutant who is able to generate and control magnetic fields. The horrors of racism and violence that he experienced as a former Jewish concentration camp prisoner shapes his outlook on life as a mutant, an outlook that rejects the idea of a peaceful mutant-human coexistence. Being Professor X's longtime friend, he has vacillated in roles ranging from supervillain to antihero to superhero. While he has helped the X-Men from time to time over the years, he refuses to believe as Professor X does that humans will accept mutants and live with them in peace. His heart is hard and bitter.

Most people have encountered others who could be characterized as having a hardened heart. Perhaps that hard-hearted person is the one you see when gazing into a mirror. How does a person's heart become calloused and unfeeling, devoid of love, hope, and joy? Sometimes it's due to outside forces such as an unexpected disease or health crisis. At other times, reckless people careen into others' lives bringing havoc and pain. Lastly, some develop hardened-hearts due to their own poor choices and the horrendous ramifications that follow. Among the negative effects that a hardened heart produces in a person's life are fear, bitterness, resentment, hatred, and loneliness.

Professor X's compassion and hope for Magneto offers a glimpse into God's great love and hope for humanity. John 3:16 confirms the fact that God does not think people are a lost cause and worth giving up on: "For God so loved the world that he gave his one and only Son, that whoever believes in him shall not perish but have eternal life." God's love can soften any hard heart.

Look, Up In the Sky…

Revelation 1:4-8

> [4] *John, To the seven churches in the province of Asia: Grace and peace to you from him who is, and who was, and who is to come, and from the seven spirits before his throne,* [5] *and from Jesus Christ, who is the faithful witness, the firstborn from the dead, and the ruler of the kings of the earth. To him who loves us and has freed us from our sins by his blood,* [6] *and has made us to be a kingdom and priests to serve his God and Father—to him be glory and power forever and ever! Amen.* [7] *"Look, he is coming with the clouds," and "every eye will see him, even those who pierced him; and*

all the peoples of the earth will mourn because of him." So shall it be! Amen. [8] *"I am the Alpha and the Omega," says the Lord God, "who is, and who was, and who is to come, the Almighty."*

* **Revelation 1:4-8** → John wrote this letter (book of Revelation) initially to the seven churches that are addressed in chapters 2 and 3, all geographically located in modern-day Turkey. He reminds his readers and hearers of this foundational truth: that the Lord Jesus Christ loves the world and has offered freedom from both the power and penalty of sin by laying down his life and shedding his blood for mankind. There is an eternal kingdom to come that is glorious beyond comprehension. Jesus will be glorified forever and ever as the Ruler of this eternal dominion. Will you be there? Have you surrendered to him?

Regardless of who has or hasn't surrendered to him, nothing will slow down the Lord Jesus Christ's imminent return to earth. Read verses 7 and 8, recognizing that he is the Alpha (first letter in the Greek alphabet) and the Omega (last letter in the Greek alphabet) – words that speak to his eternal existence. He is before all things and the end of all things. He is not a boss. He is *the Boss*, the Almighty One! Now you know from where the comic book writers got some of their ideas and wording when they wrote statements for the character Apocalypse.

Chapter 3

The Voice...Like a Trumpet

Revelation 1:9-11

Cable: "It's called the Lazarus Chamber...it's the secret to Apocalypse's longevity. He goes into hibernation there every hundred years."

[X-Men The Animated Series: Beyond Good and Evil (Part 3)]

Apocalypse needs a rejuvenation device, referred to as the Lazarus Chamber in the animated series, to allow him to "live eternally". The chamber is equated to an ancient Egyptian sarcophagus (the coffins where deceased Egyptian pharaohs were placed). This fictitious chamber puts Apocalypse in suspended animation for long periods of time and also allows him to heal. Thus, he has the perceived ability to live forever.

In reality, however, it is the Lord Jesus Christ who is the eternal One that has all power. And not only is he the forever-living One, but he is able to grant eternal life to all who trust him. By the way, do you know where comic writers got the name "Lazarus"? From the Bible, of course. Lazarus was a man who died and, after four days of being buried in a tomb, Jesus came and brought him back to life. Check out John 11:1-45 (for those not familiar with the Bible, that's chapter 11, verses 1 through 45).

This is *The* Voice

Revelation 1:9-11

> [9] *I, John, your brother and companion in the suffering and kingdom and patient endurance that are ours in Jesus, was on the island of Patmos because of the word of God and the testimony of Jesus.* [10] *On the Lord's Day I was in the Spirit, and I heard behind me a loud voice like a trumpet,* [11] *which said: "Write on a scroll what you see and send it to the seven churches: to Ephesus, Smyrna, Pergamum, Thyatira, Sardis, Philadelphia and Laodicea."*

* Revelation 1:9 → Most things in life that are deemed valuable and of high worth will cost much to acquire. How much more the eternal riches of God. We live in an age of "cheap grace"; an era in which people want the bounty of God with little-to-no effort, devotion, obedience, or commitment. John wrote this verse with the words "suffering", "kingdom", and "patient endurance" all linked together. He knew something about these words. He had been exiled by Rome's emperor, Domitian, to Patmos, a barren and desolate small island in the Aegean Sea, off the west coast of Turkey and the continent of Asia.

Domitian was cruelly violent, blatantly deviant in immoral living and sexual lusts, and demanded to be worshiped as God. He despised Christians and had them killed. Tradition indicates that Domitian first tried to kill John by boiling him in oil, but John miraculously lived. Rather than kill him another way and inadvertently make him a martyr, Domitian exiled John to Patmos and hoped his influence would fade away. Domitian was wrong. John remained faithful to the word of God and the testimony of Jesus.

How about you? To what or whom are you committed? At the end of your life when you prepare to step into eternity, the only real commitment that will matter is commitment to the One of whom the Apocalypse is revealing – the Great Lord of the universe, Jesus Christ.

MUTANT INSIGHT

Apocalypse: "This is where your power was born – and this is where your people were slaughtered."
Magneto: "You shouldn't have brought me here."
Apocalypse: "Why? Are you afraid to be here? You can't escape it Erik."

[X-Men: Apocalypse]

Apocalypse attempts to trigger deep-seeded anger in Magento's heart and, thereby, unleash his full and unbridled power to bring about global destruction on the earth. This would accomplish Apocalypse's demented purposes. How does he aim to do this? By taking Magneto to the Auschwitz concentration camp where his Jewish relatives and kinsmen were sadistically exterminated during Adolph Hitler's bid to rule the world. Magneto affirms that being in that place of bad memories, pain, and death will cause him to unleash his fury. Under the guise of taking Magneto to the camp to free him of his fears, Apocalypse actually wants to bind him in new shackles of poor decision-making – even cause him in blind wrath to use his power to exterminate and, inadvertently, do to others what he claims makes him hate Auschwitz.

Beyond the world of fiction, we must be careful to not allow unresolved conflict, bitterness, and/or anger to be used by others for their ends and our downfall. The Bible's admonition is to,

> See to it that no one falls short of the grace of God
> and that no bitter root grows up to cause trouble
> and defile many. [Hebrew 12:15]

Only God can free people from deep fears and bondages that either openly or secretly keep them from living lives of true peace, faith, hope, and love. How is it possible to conquer debilitating fear, anger, lust and other chains of darkness?

> Repent, then, and turn to God, so that your sins may
> be wiped out, that times of refreshing may come
> from the Lord, and that he may send the Messiah,
> who has been appointed for you--even Jesus. [Acts
> 3:19-20]

---

* **Revelation 1:10-11** → "The Lord's Day" was the term the early disciples of Jesus used to refer to the first day of the week (Sunday). In contrast, "The Day of the Lord" is a phrase used in the Bible to refer to the Day on which Jesus Christ will come to the earth a second time, not as the sacrificial Lamb to be slain, but as the Lion that will conquer. John's statement that he "was in the Spirit" is a reference to the fact that he was translated into the spiritual realm (whether in body or just spirit is not clear) to see and hear what the Lord Jesus wanted to reveal to him. Have you ever heard a trumpet blast? The sound of the majestic and awe-filled voice of the Lord Jesus can be compared to the experience of the Jewish people in the Old Testament who heard God's voice. Consider the following two passages of Scripture that describe God's voice as a trumpet:

> ...there was thunder and lightning, with a thick
> cloud over the mountain, and a very loud trumpet
> blast. Everyone in the camp trembled. Then Moses

led the people out of the camp to meet with God, and they stood at the foot of the mountain. Mt. Sinai was covered with smoke, because the LORD descended on it in fire. The smoke billowed up from it like smoke from a furnace, the whole mountain trembled violently…" [Exodus 19:16-18]

and

When the people saw the thunder and lighting and heard the trumpet and saw the mountain in smoke, they trembled with fear. They stayed at a distance and said to Moses, "Speak to us yourself and we will listen. But do not have God speak to us or we will die.' Moses said the people, 'Do not be afraid. God has come to test you, so that the fear [reverence] of God will be with you to keep you from sinning.'" [Exodus 20:16-20]

Chapter 4

The Vision of the Living One

Revelation 1:12-20

Apocalypse: "I am far beyond mutants as they are above you. I am eternal."

[X-Men The Animated Series: Time Fugitives, Part 1]

T he words stated above by Apocalypse are actually fulfilled in real life by the Lord Jesus Christ. He is eternal, immortal, and unequaled in power, glory, and majesty. The great news is that he loves all people – yes, even the most rebellious among us who thinks and cares nothing about him. Keep reading to learn more about His love, offer of forgiveness of sins, and willingness to reconcile you to himself. As a side note, the pantheon of superheroes in both Marvel and DC comics feature one being (in each comic line) who is considered to be God. Marvel has given him the name the "One-Above-All". Over the years, Marvel comic creators and writers have expressed the following to their readers about God:

> Apparently responsible for the existence of all life in the Multiverse and possibly beyond, the One-Above-All is the master and sole superior of the cosmic overseer and arbitrator known as the Living Tribunal, whose faces, embodying Equity, Vengeance

and Necessity respectively, are in perfect alignment with one another as it passes judgment…When the pregnant Susan Storm feared for her husband's possible death at the hands of the "all-powerful" Silver Surfer, Uatu the Watcher tells her that there is only one being that is truly "all-powerful", and that *"His only weapon…is love!"* During an encounter with the Sorcerer Supreme Doctor Strange, the cosmic entity Eternity tells Strange: "I and my brother, Death, comprise all of your reality, mystic! Neither he nor I are God, for God rules *all* realities!" When Thor once compared himself and Odin to various other gods and abstract beings in terms of power, he notes: "…and 'tis said that a being, called the Living Tribunal—the final judge—hath the power to enforce his will 'pon any cosmos he doth judge! And 'tis said his power is supreme in all the Multiverse. Even I, son of one of the mightiest of all gods, find it impossible to conceive of such levels of power! And 'tis a humbling thought to consider how much greater the Creator of all Universes must be than that of *all* of His creations combined!"

http://marvel.wikia.com/wiki/One-Above-ll_%28Multiverse%29

Stars, Lampstands, and the One Like No Other

Revelation 1:12-20

[12] *I turned around to see the voice that was speaking to me. And when I turned I saw seven golden lampstands,* [13] *and among the lampstands was*

someone "like a son of man," dressed in a robe reaching down to his feet and with a golden sash around his chest. [14] His head and hair were white like wool, as white as snow, and his eyes were like blazing fire. [15] His feet were like bronze glowing in a furnace, and his voice was like the sound of rushing waters. [16] In his right hand he held seven stars, and out of his mouth came a sharp double-edged sword. His face was like the sun shining in all its brilliance. [17] When I saw him, I fell at his feet as though dead. Then he placed his right hand on me and said: "Do not be afraid. I am the First and the Last. [18] I am the Living One; I was dead, and behold I am alive forever and ever! And I hold the keys of death and Hades. [19] "Write, therefore, what you have seen, what is now and what will take place later. [20] The mystery of the seven stars that you saw in my right hand and of the seven golden lampstands is this: The seven stars are the angels of the seven churches, and the seven lampstands are the seven churches.

* **Revelation 1:12-13** → What are the seven golden lampstands mentioned in verse twelve? Verse twenty provides the answer: They represent the seven churches that Jesus addresses in the next two chapters. The state of these seven historical churches also speak to the spiritual condition of any church (congregation of believers) or individuals who acknowledge Jesus as their Lord and Savior. The purpose of a lampstand is to hold/give forth light. Thus, the seven golden lampstands are symbolic of the followers of Christ within each church radiating the light and glory of Christ. Consider these words of Jesus to his disciples:

> You are the light of the world. A town built on a hill
> cannot be hidden. Neither do people light a lamp
> and put it under a bowl. Instead they put it on its
> stand, and it gives light to everyone in the house. In
> the same way, let your light shine before others, that
> they may see your good deeds and glorify your Fa-
> ther in heaven. [Matthew 5:14-16]

 * **Revelation 1:14-15** → The word "like" is a simile, a figure
of speech that draws a comparison between two different things.
John uses the word "like" in these verses to do his best (with the
language of man) to describe his vision of the eternal God and
Savior, Jesus Christ – in his glorified body. The white hair speaks
to his wisdom and eternality. His eyes, blazing like fire, indicate
that he sees all things – burning through the façades, masks,
pretensions, and deceptions that many live with on a daily basis,
fooling all around them except God himself. The Bible has this to
say about the blazing and all-seeing eyes of the Lord:

> Nothing in all creation is hidden from God's sight.
> Everything is uncovered and laid bare before the
> eyes of him to whom we must give account. [He-
> brews 4:13]

What this means is that no one can find a hiding place from
the everywhere-present and all-knowing Lord of the universe.
And know this: He is not watching people only because he's
looking for their faults. While he is aware of all sin, even before
people commit them, he is looking at each person for only one
primary reason: because he loves them. He is watching people
with the hope that they will acknowledge their need for him as
their sin- bearer, Savior, Counselor, Friend, and Master.

John's description of Jesus' feet, which looked like bronze
glowing in a furnace, speaks of Jesus' purity, high worth, and

hardness regarding his foes. During John's day and the writing of Revelation (approximately A.D. 96), bronze was considered one of the most important alloys (a mixture of tin and copper). Bronze was to that historical era what fictitious metals such as Adamantium (an indestructible metal alloy that is bonded to Wolverine's bones and claws) and Vanadium (a metal that is able to absorb all soundwaves, vibrations, and kinetic energy, found in Captain America's shield) are in the comic world. Think about the contrast between the X-Men character Colossus' normal body of flesh versus his transformed metal body. John's description of Jesus' glorified body, with feet like bronze and blazing splendor, provided readers and hearers of that time period with a vivid contrast between Jesus' powerful and majestic resurrected body and his earthly body of flesh and blood that had been crucified.

* **Revelation 1:16** → What are the seven stars mentioned here? As with the seven lampstands, Revelation 1:20 provides the answer. They are the seven angels of the seven churches Jesus will talk about in chapters two and three. The word angel is the Greek word "angelos" and is translated "messenger". The sharp double-edged sword that comes out of Jesus' mouth is his all-powerful and irresistible word. Think about this, with one word or gesture, many human leaders have the authority and power to command others to act. With artificial intelligence, we can speak to machines and they fulfill our wishes. How much greater the eternal and majestic word of God, who is able to have all things in the universe submit to his will.

MUTANT INSIGHT

Magneto: "Who are you?"
Apocalypse: "Elohim, Pushan, Ra. I've been called many names over many lifetimes. I am born of death. I was there to spark

and fan the flame of mankind's awakening – to spin the wheel of civilization. And when the forest would grow rank and needed clearing for new growth, I was there to set it ablaze."

[X-Men: Apocalypse]

Without question, Apocalypse has a definite god-complex. When Magneto asks who he is, Apocalypse boasts that people over many centuries have related him to various deities – though the ones he lists are very different.

In the Hebrew Bible, Elohim is translated as the God of Israel and means the "Mighty One". Elohim is the name God ascribes to himself in the book of Genesis – as the Creator of the universe and mankind. Elohim, the God of the Bible, has no other gods before him.

Pushan is one of twelve solar deities in Hinduism and one of thousands in Hindu's pantheon of gods. He is not supreme like the God of the Bible and is an offspring of Aditi, the mother of the gods. As a sun god, he was a god of meeting and a supportive guide, leading dedicated followers towards rich pastures and wealth. Again, far from being deemed supreme, he supposedly had his teeth knocked out by another god (the story varies within Hinudism as to who knocked his teeth out). Lastly, one major differentiation between Pushan and the holy god of the Bible is Pushan's relationship with his sister, Dawn (the avatar of the sun). Dawn is referred to as Pushan's lover. Yikes! Incest, losing fights to other gods,…not a god one should desire to follow.

Ra is the ancient Egyptian sun god and one of many deities in Egypt's pantheon. Early dynasties associated him with the noon sun. Later Egyptian dynasties merged Ra with the god Horus (the fictional son of Isis and Osiris). In this belief system, Ra called all forms of life into existence by calling their secret name. Man, however, was supposedly created from Ra's tears and sweat. The

Egyptian's worship of Ra died out with the rise of Christianity, making today's study of Ra primarily academic.

Now you should have a better understanding of the true and radical differences between the God of the Bible and other deities. For Apocalypse to call himself all three names above is like a person today referring to their mobile phone and declaring that it has three different brands and/or three different carriers. This is impossible because no two mobile phone companies are the same and no customer receives service from one company yet pays another the bill for service. In the same way, all deities are not the same. The apostle Paul touches on this in Acts 17:16-31

Lastly, the truth of Apocalypse's existence in the fictional comic world is that he is a finite being, a mutant born in a coastal city in southern Jordan. He has been able to live over many centuries by using his mutant power to transfer his consciousness to other host-bodies, before his previous one died from old age. This occurred in the opening scene of the movie. Also, by way of his hibernation chamber and time travel technology, he appears to be an infinite being to others. Thus, he over-exaggerates (actually, he is lying) when he tells Magneto that he was present at mankind's creation, spinning the wheel of civilization. Sadly, this type of interaction between Apocalypse and Magneto is played out every day in real life. People over-inflate their credentials and abilities to gain approval, qualify for opportunities, and obtain things that they want. Many times, however, charlatans are revealed for who they really are, being eventually exposed as cheaters, liars, and not qualified.

---

* **Revelation 1:17-18** → In these verses, John was flat-out overwhelmed with wonder, awe, and fear as he stood before Jesus, the resurrected Ruler and Judge of the Universe. Did you know that every person who is either living today, has already

died, or has yet to be born will one day stand before this Judge and be called to give an account of their lives? For those who do not yet know him as their personal Savior and Lord, that judgment day will be a day of eternal sadness, regret, and doom. If you have not yet done so, why not surrender to Jesus' love and Kingship today. Implore others to do the same. His second coming and reign on earth is imminent.

The reference to Jesus being the First and the Last speaks to him being eternal in existence. He is before all things and is the end of all things. He is God. Scripture tells us that prior to Jesus' resurrection from the dead, Hades (or Sheol in Hebrew) was where all people's souls went when their bodies died [see Luke 16:19-31]. Ever since Jesus' resurrection, the only souls that go to Hades are those of people who reject Jesus as who he professes to be: Savior and Lord. People who confess their sin and place their hope in the Lord Jesus Christ as the only qualified sin-bearer and Savior don't go to Hades when they die. Rather, they go straight to heaven. The souls in Hades will remain there until judgment day. After their court hearing before the Judge, they will be cast into the eternal lake of fire, also referred to as hell (in the Greek language, the word is Gehenna). This will be discussed later in this book, in the review of Revelation 20.

Satan runs neither Hades nor Gehenna. On the contrary, he will one day be cast into this eternal place to be tormented day and night. Who has the keys to death and hell? It is Jesus. He is the ruler of all. Hollywood and other mediums of communication have led many to believe erroneous things when it comes to God, spirituality, and eternity. Satan will one day be crushed by Jesus. And be sure, Jesus could do it now if He so chose, but He will do it at the appointed time. Read the Bible, submit to Jesus' lordship, and live life for his glory.

* **Revelation 1:19** → Jesus, having told John to "snap out of it", like He did to Moses [see Exodus 4], now tells him to do what he has been called to do for God's glory and the benefit of

mankind. This message is applicable to us today. God commands all people who have submitted to Jesus to not make excuses and tremble in fear with regard to His call and purposes for their lives. Rather, he commands them to trust him, embrace His love, and walk in the power and calling he has given them. Do you feel God tugging on your heart to do something for him? Perhaps it's sharing the love and truth of God with a co-worker, family member, or friend. Whatever it is that you hear him calling you to do, be bold and trust him. He is the God of unlimited power and great expectations. You may not have super-powers, but he has promised to empower all who are willing to seek him and walk in obedience to Him.

* Revelation 1:20 → As discussed earlier, the word "angel" is translated "messenger". This word can apply to angelic heavenly beings or human messengers. Many Bible scholars believe that these seven messengers to the seven churches spoken of in Revelation 2 and 3 were angles assigned to the churches. Others believe that these messengers were the churches' pastors. If that was the case, then the description of them as stars has a direct connection to the scriptural references of those who teach and live out God's truths to others:

> Those who are wise (impart wisdom to others) will shine like the brightness of the heavens, and those who lead many to righteousness, like the stars for ever and ever. [Daniel 12:3]

> Do everything without complaining or arguing, so that you may become blameless and pure, children of God without fault in a crooked and depraved generation, in which you shine like stars in the universe as you hold out the word of life… [Phil. 2:14-16(a)]

Many people want to be stars in this world, pursuing fame and riches in various fields such as entertainment, sports, and business. While they may receive applause from thousands or even millions of people, the applause of people means nothing if their lives are not applauded by God. The Bible makes it clear that God examines the lives of all people. Those whose lives shine like stars before God are those who obey him, live wisely and instruct others in the way of truth and righteousness. We've already discussed that the seven churches referenced in this verse, to be examined in the next two chapters, were located in the land now referred to as Turkey. What is important to know and remember is that when the Bible speaks of the church, it is not referring to buildings or man-made denominations. The word "church" is the translation of the following Greek word (language of the New Testament) *ekklesia*:

> **ekklesia** – from ek, meaning "out of", and klesis, meaning "a calling".

Thus, the meaning of the word "church" refers to the assembly of followers of Christ who have trusted him as their Savior and Lord. He redeems and calls out – from the general population of the earth who reject his lordship and sovereign rule – all who trust in Him. So one's eternal destiny is inextricably linked to their decision to either accept or reject Jesus as their Master and Lord.

Chapter 5

So Who's Your First Love?

Revelation 2:1-7

Jean Grey: "You've given us a place where we belong, Professor."
Rogue: "Just takes us hard-headed ones longer to realize it."

[X-Men The Animated Series: Come the Apocalypse]

T he statements of these two fictional mutant characters are addressed to Professor X, who has taken them into his care and mentorship. Each of their sentiments contain realities that are applicable to all of us as pertaining to God and our response to him. God loves all people and desires to adopt them into his family if they are willing to turn to him in repentance of sins. The apostle John, who recorded the book of Revelation, makes this clear in the first chapter of the book of John (fourth book of the New Testament), which he also inscribed:

> Yet to all who did receive him [Jesus], to those who believed in his name, he gave the right to become children of God— children born not of natural descent, nor of human decision or a husband's will, but born of God. [John 1:12,13]

The question God poses to everyone is this: are you willing to trust him and accept his offer of love, forgiveness, acceptance, and transformation? Just as they do in the lives of super-powered comic characters, the forces of good and evil pull at people every day. Each person must choose which they will serve. As Rogue states above, let's not be hard-headed and keep resisting the call of truth, righteousness, and honor. Rather, just as the X-Men willfully became Professor X's disciples, submit to God's call to follow him, obey him, and experience the peace, joy, hope, and love that he offers.

Get Refocused On the Main Thing

Revelation 2:1-7

> [1] *"To the angel of the church in Ephesus write: These are the words of him who holds the seven stars in his right hand and walks among the seven golden lampstands:* [2] *I know your deeds, your hard work and your perseverance. I know that you cannot tolerate wicked men, that you have tested those who claim to be apostles but are not, and have found them false.* [3] *You have persevered and have endured hardships for my name, and have not grown weary.* [4] *Yet I hold this against you: You have forsaken your first love.* [5] *Remember the height from which you have fallen! Repent and do the things you did at first. If you do not repent, I will come to you and remove your lampstand from its place.* [6] *But you have this in your favor: You hate the practices of the Nicolaitans, which I also hate.* [7] *He who has an ear, let him hear what the Spirit says to the churches. To him who overcomes, I will give the right to eat*

from the tree of life, which is in the paradise of God.

* **Revelation 2:1** → The first words of this verse pertain to John being commanded by Jesus to write down his [Jesus'] words of encouragement, rebuke, and instruction. These were to be given to the "messenger" (pastor) of the church in Ephesus, who would, in turn, share them with the congregation. Each year, millions of children learn and sing the song, "He's Got the Whole World In His Hands". Maybe you've heard the song and even sang it as a child. God, indeed, holds everything in order and controls everything by his power and sovereign rule. More specifically and intimately, the Lord Jesus holds the church (defined in the Bible as the entire collection of all who have surrendered to his lordship) in his all-powerful hand. He dwells with all-knowledge among those who are his. Exponentially more than the fictitious Professor X, Jesus can be completely trusted as Savior, Counselor, and Friend!

Ephesus was the wealthiest and greatest city in the Roman province of Asia. It also had wide-spread occult practices and was the center of worship for the idol Artemis (Diana of the Ephesians). The temple of Artemis was the site of rampant crime and immorality with hundreds of priestesses serving as "sacred" prostitutes. Its economy was based on superstitions with people traveling to Ephesus from all over the world in order to purchase amulets and charms that were supposed to heal people of various ailments and issues.

* **Revelation 2:2-4** → The Lord Jesus commended his followers who lived in Ephesus for many good things that they were doing for the kingdom of God. They were committed to working hard to uphold standards of truth and righteousness. They had persevered through trials thrown at them by God-haters. Jesus also praised them for not tolerating wicked people and working to eradicate their influence. However, he told the

Ephesians that what they were doing was worthless before him if done in their own power and not focused on a love relationship with him. This is akin to a man who buys his wife flowers, jewelry, and clothes each week yet spends no time with her. If she really loves him, then receiving all of those things without his love means nothing. Presents without presence is empty.

PAUSE:

> *This is what's so great about the parallel between the message of the Bible and the fictional superhero genre.* The superheroes that millions around the world flock to see in the movies, online, on television, and in comics are revered because they, too, hate the deeds of wicked people and work hard to eliminate evil's influence. But think about this: many people reject Jesus and his call to live righteously *yet* they love spending their time and money watching fictional heroes live righteously, fight against wickedness, and uphold truth...Now, back to Jesus and his critique of his followers in Ephesus.

* **Revelation 2:5** → The phrase "remember the height from which you have fallen" is Jesus' call to the Ephesians to understand that the highest position anyone can have with someone else is to be in a loving and respectful relationship. They fell from that position, becoming distanced in devotion to God because of other priorities and distractions. Again, most people can relate to this in their relationships with people they love. Maybe it's because of work, school, recreational pursuits, etc., but anyone can become distanced from loved ones over time due to not spending quality time with them.

Similarly, with respect to spiritual matters and a thriving relationship with the Lord, believers in Christ have to guard against becoming enamored with anything or anyone that interferes with sincerely loving and spending time with the Lord. It is critical to guard against becoming spiritually puffed up or forgetting that it is only by grace that one's vile motives, thoughts, words, and deeds have been forgiven. The words, "remove your lampstand" refers to Jesus no longer walking in fellowship with that institutional church and distancing himself from the error of the people making up the church. In contrast, to live the most joyous, peaceful, and purpose-led life, followers of Jesus must walk daily in humility, seeking to know Him in an ever-deepening relationship.

MUTANT INSIGHT

Nightcrawler: "So all people are flawed and all struggle with the capacity for sin. None likes to be reminded of our shared human weakness."

[X-Men The Animated Series: Nightcrawler]

Are you finally at a place in your life when you can acknowledge that you, too, are flawed and not perfect? Did you know that the word "sin" – used in the Bible to define anything that violates the ideal relationship between us and God – has its origins in archery? Yes, Hawkeye and Katinas Everdeen fans, its true! In archery, the word "sin" refers to missing the "gold" (bulls-eye) at the center of a target and, instead, hitting any other spot on the target. Archers call not hitting the target at all as "a miss". The center of the target represents perfection. We all miss that mark. Yes, that includes you, me, and every person ever born since Adam and Eve's rebellion in the garden of Eden. Keep reading to discover God's redemptive plans to rescue us from the penalty of sin, which is eternal punishment.

---

* **Revelation 2:6** → God is loving and patient. Thus, he balances his rebuke and warning in Revelation 2:5 with additional words of commendation in this verse. Jesus hated the ungodly practices of the Nicolatians – and so did the church of Ephesus. In the original Greek language, the word "Nicolatians" is made up of two words: *nikao* – meaning "to conquer" and *laos* – meaning "people".

The word Nicolatians has nearly the identical meaning to the Hebrew word Baalam – meaning "destroyer of the people" or "confuser of the people". Balaam was an Old Testament prophet who fell into greed and spiritual wickedness by sabotaging the Israelites as they entered the promised land. According to Numbers 31:16 and Revelation 2:14, Balaam sided with one of Israel's enemies, Balak, king of Moab (modern day central-western Jordan), advising the king how to coerce the Israelites to curse themselves (lose God's favor). Balaam told Balak to entice the Israelites with prostitutes and eat food sacrificed to idols. The Israelites fell into these sinful traps and, as a result, God sent a deadly plague upon them.

> While Israel was staying in Shittim, the men began to indulge in sexual immorality with Moabite women, who invited them to the sacrifices to their gods. The people ate the sacrificial meal and bowed down before these gods. So Israel yoked themselves to the Baal of Peor. And the Lord's anger burned against them. The Lord said to Moses, "Take all the leaders of these people, kill them and expose them in broad daylight before the Lord, so that the Lord's fierce

anger may turn away from Israel." So Moses said to Israel's judges, "Each of you must put to death those of your people who have yoked themselves to the Baal of Peor. [Numbers 25:1-5]

Moses was angry with the officers of the army—the commanders of thousands and commanders of hundreds—who returned from the battle. 'Have you allowed all the women to live?' he asked them. "They were the ones who followed Balaam's advice and enticed the Israelites to be unfaithful to the LORD in the Peor incident, so that a plague struck the LORD's people. [Numbers 31:14-16]

The Nicolatians professed to be followers of Jesus but lived in sensuality and rebellion to God's commands pertaining to sexual purity and spiritual obedience. They also encouraged others to engage in similar rebellion.

* **Revelation 2:7** → Question: With all that you hear on a daily basis, whether at work, school, recreation, E-mail, phone, text, etc, are you hearing (and more importantly, listening to) God and his Word? Many know about the lives of celebrities, lyrics to pop hits, and headlines in world news, but are not living with such purpose as to know what God says. They are thus not overcoming the influence, power, and consequences of wickedness? It is a choice. Later, the review of Revelation 22 will look at the tree of life and God's paradise. But please don't hesitate to read it before then!

Chapter 6

Kanye's Right: The Devil's Tryin' To Break Us Down

Revelation 2:8-11

Nightcrawler: "…but then I found peace by devoting my life to God. He directed me to this place, where they judge me by the character of my heart, not my appearance."

[X-Men The Animated Series: Nightcrawler]

Whether one is rich and famous or poor and barely known, everyone wants peace, contentment, acceptance, and love. These are the things our hearts long for, and no amount of fortune, fame, or talents will bestow the highest level of these treasured gifts. No, it is only by dedicating one's life to God that we can truly begin to experience the life that Jesus speaks about in John 10:10-11:

> The thief comes only to steal and kill and destroy;
> I have come that they may have life, and have it to
> the full. I am the good shepherd. The good shepherd
> lays down his life for the sheep.

The life Jesus describes first brings peace between sinners and God. Second, it brings inner peace in this life, regardless of what is happening externally. But Satan, referred to as Lucifer prior to his spiritual rebellion in heaven, has always used deceptive promises to cause people to compromise truth and reject God for the sake of pleasure and temporal gain. So don't buy the lies of the television series, *Lucifer*, which premiered in 2016. He is not kind, does not care about you, and only wants to kill, steal, and destroy.

Don't Be Afraid...Trust Him and Remain Faithful

Revelation 2:8-11

> [8] *To the angel of the church in Smyrna write: These are the words of him who is the First and the Last, who died and came to life again.* [9] *I know your afflictions and your poverty—yet you are rich! I know the slander of those who say they are Jews and are not, but are a synagogue of Satan.* [10] *Do not be afraid of what you are about to suffer. I tell you, the devil will put some of you in prison to test you, and you will suffer persecution for ten days. Be faithful, even to the point of death, and I will give you the crown of life.* [11] *He who has an ear, let him hear what the Spirit says to the churches. He who overcomes will not be hurt at all by the second death.*

* **Revelation 2:8** → Let the words of this verse sink into your heart, mind, and life-choices. Jesus is the Eternal One, the First and the Last. He was not merely a nice man and a good teacher. He is before all things and the end of all things. Even after he willingly submitted himself to be crucified (capital punishment) and took upon himself the punishment for the world's sin, Jesus proved that he is the resurrection and the life, able to not only raise himself from the dead, but also grant eternal life to all who trust in him.

* **Revelation 2:9** → Smyrna (modern day Izmir in Turkey) had a segment of the population who claimed to be Jewish, but were not – Satanic in operations and hostile towards Christians. The city itself was devoted to Roman emperor worship. This too made it dangerous for believers in Jesus to be open about their faith. A result of this persecution from both the false Jews and Gentiles (non-Jews) was extreme financial hardships for the Christians of Smyrna. The Jewish synagogue was referred to as the "synagogue of Satan" because they were not spiritually of God's family [see Romans 2:17-29], but belonged to Satan [see John 8:42-47]. The word *satan* means "adversary". This adversary, who desires that people reject God and spend eternity in hell, is far more powerful than any human. He is the "dark force" behind both wicked men in the real world and evil characters in the fictional world. His power is beyond our imagination. And yet, his power compared to Jesus' power is like comparing a 9-volt battery's power output to that of the sun. No comparison at all!

* **Revelation 2:10-11** → The word "devil" (from Greek word *diabolos*) means "accuser" or "slanderer". Jesus calls the devil "the father of lies" [John 8:44]. The Lord encourages, yes, even commands, all who follow him not to be afraid when they endure sufferings for obeying and exalting him. Better to be rejected by man for living to please Jesus than to be rejected by Jesus for living to please man:

> When the Son of Man comes in his glory, and all the
> angels with him, he will sit on his glorious throne.
> All the nations will be gathered before him, and
> he will separate the people one from another as a
> shepherd separates the sheep from the goats. He
> will put the sheep on his right and the goats on his

left. "Then the King will say to those on his right, 'Come, you who are blessed by my Father; take your inheritance, the kingdom prepared for you since the creation of the world. For I was hungry and you gave me something to eat, I was thirsty and you gave me something to drink, I was a stranger and you invited me in, I needed clothes and you clothed me, I was sick and you looked after me, I was in prison and you came to visit me.' "Then the righteous will answer him, 'Lord, when did we see you hungry and feed you, or thirsty and give you something to drink? When did we see you a stranger and invite you in, or needing clothes and clothe you? When did we see you sick or in prison and go to visit you?' "The King will reply, 'Truly I tell you, whatever you did for one of the least of these brothers and sisters of mine, you did for me.' "Then he will say to those on his left, 'Depart from me, you who are cursed, into the eternal fire prepared for the devil and his angels. For I was hungry and you gave me nothing to eat, I was thirsty and you gave me nothing to drink, I was a stranger and you did not invite me in, I needed clothes and you did not clothe me, I was sick and in prison and you did not look after me.' "They also will answer, 'Lord, when did we see you hungry or thirsty or a stranger or needing clothes or sick or in prison, and did not help you?' "He will reply, "Truly I tell you, whatever you did not do for one of the least of these, you did not do for me.' "Then they will go away to eternal punishment, but the righteous to eternal life. [Matthew 25:31-46].

There are rewards, riches, crowns, and blessings that the human mind cannot conceive or fathom which will be bestowed upon all who overcome their fear of being Jesus' faithful witnesses and who live for his honor. Polycarp was a 2nd-century bishop of Smyrna. "According to the *Martyrdom of Polycarp,* he died a martyr, bound and burned at the stake, then stabbed when the fire failed to touch him."[2] Polycarp is recorded as saying on the day of his death about Jesus, "Eighty and six years I have served Him, and He has done me no wrong. How then can I blaspheme my King and Savior? Bring forth what thou wilt." Polycarp was burned at the stake for refusing to burn incense to the Roman Emperor". Like Polycarp, be faithful my friends; God will not fail you!

Chapter 7

Compromise: The Road of Ease and Destruction

Revelation 2:12-17

Nightcrawler: "We all feel like that sometimes. Friends can help; but in our times of loneliness we forget that we are all part of a greater family – the family of God. All other comfort is fleeting; only God endures… everyday I pray for the Lord to forgive my sins and to forgive the sins of others – even those who have done harm to me."

Jubilee: "I…don't think I could do that."

Nightcrawler: "That is why I look to God for help, because we cannot do it by ourselves. He can give you the strength to forgive."

Jubilee: "Whew, this religious stuff is intense."

[X-Men The Animated Series: Bloodlines]

Y ou might be saying to yourself, "I don't need God. My life is going okay; I have good health. I'm having fun with friends and activities. I like my job. I serve in the community to help those less fortunate…I'm good!"

Well friend, I'm sorry to break the news to you, but you won't always be healthy. Live long enough, and one day your mortal body will begin to break down with age – or some unfortunate accident. Job security is also never guaranteed. You will one day discover that your resources of time, talent, and treasure will all run out in this lifetime. Look to God today for hope, in both this temporal life and for the eternal one to come.

Surveillance: He Knows Where You Live

Revelation 2:12-17

[12] To the angel of the church in Pergamum write: These are the words of him who has the sharp, double-edged sword. [13] I know where you live— where Satan has his throne. Yet you remain true to my name. You did not renounce your faith in me, even in the days of Antipas, my faithful witness, who was put to death in your city—where Satan lives. [14] Nevertheless, I have a few things against you: You have people there who hold to the teaching of Balaam, who taught Balak to entice the Israelites to sin by eating food sacrificed to idols and by committing sexual immorality. [15] Likewise you also have those who hold to the teaching of the Nicolatians. [16] Repent therefore! Otherwise, I will soon come to you and will fight against them with the sword of my mouth. [17] He who has an ear, let him hear what the Spirit says to the churches. To him who overcomes, I will give some of the hidden manna. I will also give him a white stone with a new name written on it, known only to him who receives it.

* **Revelation 2:12** → Jesus is God incarnate, referred to in the Bible as the Word of God [read John 1:1-5,10,14]. His word is like a sharp, double-edged sword, one that cuts through all.

> For the word of God is alive and active. Sharper than any double-edged sword, it penetrates even to dividing soul and spirit, joints and marrow; it judges the thoughts and attitudes of the heart. Nothing in all creation is hidden from God's sight. Everything is uncovered and laid bare before the eyes of him to whom we must give account. [Hebrews 4:12-13].

* **Revelation 2:13** → Pergamum was the capital city of the Roman province of Asia. It was famous for its university and library, which contained more than 200,000 parchment scrolls (equivalent to books). Sadly, the accumulation of books (knowledge) does not always equate to the attainment of truth, understanding and wisdom. Pergamum rejected the truth of God's Word and was a center for many cults and even Caesar worship. The city contained a large altar to the Greek god Zeus. Its people also worshiped the god Asclepius, who they referred to as "Asclepius the Savior", a mythological Greek god of medicine. His staff, wrapped with a snake, remains a symbol of medicine today.

There were many Christians who lived in Pergamum who were committed to living for the Lord Jesus without shame or fear. Church history informs us that Antipas, referenced in this verse, was killed by the Roman Emperor Domitian by being slowly roasted in a bronze kettle. Around the globe today, many followers of Jesus are being martyred in horrendous ways. God keeps account of it all and promises to reward those who remain faithful to him – no matter the consequences.

* **Revelation 2:14-15** → After having commended the faithful in the church at Pergamum, Jesus gave the church a stern rebuke for having in its midst those who held to the teachings of Balaam (refer back to Revelation 2:6 and the information we covered about Balaam and Balak). The express intent of these people's compromise was to satisfy their sensual desires and pleasures. This rebellious desire goes against the command of God to all who have surrendered their lives to him as Savior and Lord:

> For certain individuals whose condemnation was written about long ago have secretly slipped in among you. They are ungodly people, who pervert the grace of our God into a license for immorality and deny Jesus Christ our only Sovereign and Lord…"Woe to them! They have taken the way of Cain; they have rushed for profit into Balaam's error; they have been destroyed in Korah's rebellion. [Jude 1:4,11]

> Do not love the world or anything in the world. If anyone loves the world, love for the Fatheris not in them. For everything in the world—the lust of the flesh, the lust of the eyes, and the pride of life—comes not from the Father but from the world. The world and its desires pass away, but whoever does the will of God lives forever. [I John 2:15-17]

> You adulterous people, don't you know that friendship with the world means enmity against God? Therefore, anyone who chooses to be a friend of the world becomes an enemy of God. [James 4:4]

The Nicolatians were a heretical sect that had worked out a doctrinal compromise with the pagan (godless) society. The express intent of their compromise was to please the flesh -- no different than how many people today compromise their beliefs to indulge the flesh.

MUTANT INSIGHT

Professor X [Under the mind-control of Apocalypse]: "Hear me inhabitants of this world, this is a message; a message to every man, woman, and mutant...You have lost your way...But I have returned. The day of reckoning is here...for there is nothing that you can do to stop what is coming...This message is for one reason alone: to tell the strongest among you.."

Apocalypse [Commanding Professor X what to say]: "Those with the greatest power, this earth will be yours."

Professor X [Fighting against the mind-control of Apocalypse]: "Those with the greatest power...protect those without."

Professor X [Defiantly speaking to Apocalypse]: "That's my message to the world!"

[X-Men: Apocalypse]

Long before the writers of the *X-Men: Apocalypse* movie wrote the scene above, in which Apocalypse enters Professor X's mind and causes him to say what Apocalypse wants him to say, God spoke holy words to His prophets and apostles and had them write down those words in the Bible (see II Timothy 3:16-17 and II Peter 1:20-21). All one has to do is review the daily local, state, national, and international news to agree that sin abounds and mankind has lost its way. Jesus, as promised, will one day return to the earth as Judge and Jury. God has given us the book of Revelation in a similar way as a professor, on the first day of class, would give his students clues as to the final exam coming at the end of the semester. The professor wants all his students to pass. Sadly, however, many will not take him seriously and pay no attention to the answer book.

The message that Apocalypse wanted Professor X to relay to the world is rooted in his evolutionary beliefs. The "survival of the fittest" worldview is what he believes and promotes. Thus, he wanted Professor X to say to the world's inhabitants: "If you are strong enough to survive what I'm about to do and beat out weaker humans and mutants, then you are worthy of being in my new world." Professor X defiantly goes against the mind-controlling Apocalypse and telepathically tells the world's strongest to look out for others versus just looking out for themselves.

---

* **Revelation 2:16** → Jesus is not the one with whom one should trifle. The world has been duped by the devil and led to believe that Jesus is soft and tolerant of sin. He is not. His command, "Repent therefore!" is to all. The context of this verse, as pertaining to the church at Pergamum, was regarding some of its members who were living in lewdness and lust rather than in the will of the Lord. As seen in verse thirteen, the sword with which Jesus will fight those who don't repent is his incomparable word [re-read Hebrews 4:12-13]. Did you know that Jesus is the Warrior of all warriors? You should really want to, if you have not done so, join his team. He will not lose!

* **Revelation 2:17** → It is only those who go beyond merely "hearing" Jesus (as in just hearing background noise) and actually contemplate, examine, then obey his words/commands who will be approved by him. In this verse Jesus encourages his faithful followers in Pergamum to continue fighting the good fight of faith and overcome the ungodly pressures of their era, leaning on him as their defender, avenger, protector, Savior, and God.

For those who remain faithful, Jesus promised to provide spiritual nourishment. Manna was the edible substance that

God miraculously provided to the Israelites as they wandered in the desert after escaping slavery in Egypt back in Moses' time [Exodus 16:1-36]. In this verse, when Jesus spoke of the hidden manna, he was referring to the spiritual sustenance that he would give to his faithful followers, providing life, strength, and fulfillment to their very souls.

> Jesus said to them, 'Very truly I tell you, it is not Moses who has given you the bread from heaven, but it is my Father who gives you the true bread from heaven. For the bread of God is the bread that comes down from heaven and gives life to the world.'" "Sir," they said, "always give us this bread." Then Jesus declared, "I am the bread of life. Whoever comes to me will never go hungry, and whoever believes in me will never be thirsty." [John 6:32-35]

Jesus' promise is still true today for all who faithfully follow him. Heroes, both in fiction and real life, do many valiant things to help others. But none of them have the power to give others (and even themselves) inner peace, joy, contentment, purpose, and everlasting hope. The significance of the future new name that Jesus will give to all who submit to his Lordship pertains to his intimate knowledge of each of his followers' commitment to him while on earth. The Lord gave new names to people in the Old Testament (Abram became Abraham, Jacob became Israel) and in the New Testament (Simon became Peter, Saul became Paul, John and James became known as the Sons of Thunder). These new names may also align with personalities, giftedness, abilities, and/or accomplishments, just like the origins of most fictional superheroes' names.

Chapter 8

Hold On . . . to Your Love

Revelation 2:18-29

MUTANT INSIGHT

Nightcrawler*:* "If you are indeed my brother, then I will pray to God that you find the wisdom to work through your hatred – to find strength in his love.*"*

[X-Men The Animated Series: Bloodlines]

I n this statement, Nightcrawler is referring to his half-brother Graydon Creed, a non-mutant to whom his mother, Mystique (also Nightcrawler's mom), gave birth to by way of another mutant. Mystique had given up Graydon for adoption, just as she did Nightcrawler. Despite the pain of rejection by both his mother and other people who were frightened by his appearance, Nightcrawler overcame this trauma by allowing God's love, forgiveness, and peace to dominate his heart.

Conversely, Graydon became bitter and allowed hatred to fill his heart. Many reading this book have been significantly hurt by others throughout life. Satan wants such poisons as bitterness, unforgiveness, hatred, and revenge to drive you into deeper despair and problems. In contrast, God offers a way of true escape from the pain of your past. Consider the words above and keep reading about God's revelation of freedom, joy, and peace found in Jesus.

Stop Tolerating Spiritual and Sexual Deviancy

Revelation 2:18-29

[18] *To the angel of the church in Thyatira write: These are the words of the Son of God, whose eyes are like blazing fire and whose feet are like burnished bronze.* [19] *I know your deeds, your love and faith, your service and perseverance, and that you are now doing more than you did at first.* [20] *Nevertheless, I have this against you: You tolerate that woman Jezebel, who calls herself a prophetess. By her teaching she misleads my servants into sexual immorality and the eating of food sacrificed to idols.* [21] *I have given her time to repent of her immorality, but she is unwilling.* [22] *So I will cast her on a bed of suffering, and I will make those who commit adultery with her suffer intensely, unless they repent of her ways.* [23] *I will strike her children dead. Then all the churches will know that I am he who searches hearts and minds, and I will repay each of you according to your deeds.* [24] *Now I say to the rest of you in Thyatira, to you who do not hold to her teaching and have not learned Satan's so-called deep secrets (I will not impose any other burden on you):* [25] *Only hold on to what you have until I come.* [26] *To him who overcomes and does my will to the end, I will give authority over the nations—* [27] *'He will rule them with an iron scepter; he will dash them to pieces like pottery—just as I have received authority from my Father.* [28] *I will also give him the morning star.* [29] *He who has an ear, let him hear what the Spirit says to the churches.*

* **Revelation 2:18** → The city of Thyatira was a great commercial town well-known for its manufacture of purple dye and trade in woolen goods. Just as clothing and fashion are major industries in today's world, so Thyatira in that era was a major industrial player with guilds existing for dyers, clothing manufacturers (including wool, leather, linen) and other trades. John again affirms Jesus' eternal presence, referring to his fiery vision and unstoppable, invulnerable, and irresistible power. What a picture of the King of kings (discussed in Revelation 1:14-15). He is omniscient (knows all things) and knows us thoroughly – the good, the bad, and the ugly — and yet still loves us. Wow!!

* **Revelation 2:19-23** → The Lord Jesus Christ commends the church in Thyatira for being solid in love, serving the needy and growing in its impact. However, he also says that while they weren't yet compromising within the church, they were tolerating wickedness in the culture. It's like a police department doing its job but overlooking a crime syndicate that is doing evil things in one corner of town.

In the case of Thyatira, Jesus calls out the evil presence and activities that the church (his followers) were ignoring and not confronting. The woman Jezebel was a false prophetess, a desperately wicked and misleading teacher who taught people to practice sexual immorality, witchcraft, and idolatry. Her influence had become ingrained in the culture and practices of Thyatira, even intertwined in business procedures. People associated their success with idols, mythical gods and engaged in sensual "worship" ceremonies to sacrifice to these pagan gods. If a person did not want to participate in these ceremonies, they would be ostracized and/or persecuted. Their daily lives and even being employed became almost impossible. Thus, many Christians began compromising their faith and allegiance to God's standards.

In our culture today, there are many "Jezebels" who are doing the same things this woman did two thousand years ago. One simply needs to tune in to various forms of media to see and hear the blasphemous influence leading youth and adults astray. Remember, the undeniable truth is that superheroes *always* speak out and act against violations of truth, justice, morality, and law. Where are the voices of everyday people who abhor the garbage we see and hear? Where is the voice of the church? Why is the church (in various cities across America) so silent?

God expects the church to be the vanguard of truth. And remember, the Bible's definition of the church pertains to a group of people, not man-made buildings or man-made religious groups. The church is the collective group of people who have been forgiven of sins and reconciled to God by the sacrificial death of the Lord Jesus Christ. God calls these people to engage wickedness with the sword of the Spirit, which is the truth of the Word of God [Ephesians 6:17]. This should be done with great conviction and even greater love. All of Jezebel's children (those who follow her teachings) will be judged. FACT: If one does not know Jesus as Lord and Savior, they will only know him as Judge.

MUTANT INSIGHT

Apocalypse: "I am the rocks of the eternal shore. Crash against me and be broken!"

[X-Men The Animated Series: Obsession]

These words of Apocalypse are an adaptation from the following words of Jesus: "Anyone who falls on this stone will be broken to pieces; anyone on whom it falls will be crushed."

[Matthew 21:44] What Jesus means in referencing people being broken to pieces is this: anyone who willingly comes to him in repentance and surrenders to his lordship will experience a breaking of their own will – that is their former way of life (sin-driven). Jesus will re-build them from the inside-out. Conversely, those who refuse to surrender to Jesus' lordship and continue walking in defiance will one day be crushed. For all eternity, they will endure the consequences of unforgiveness of their sin and not being reconciled to God.

---

* **Revelation 2:24-25** → The so-called "deep secrets of Satan" that were being taught by the lady operating in the spirit of Jezebel, when John wrote these verses, were rooted in an anti-biblical philosophy: the religion of Gnosticism. This satanic system of beliefs teaches that salvation comes by learning esoteric spiritual "truths" (supposedly hidden knowledge and/or spiritual secrets intended to be understood by only an initiated few) which will free humanity from the material world. This religious movement believes the material world, including the physical body, to be evil. Pay attention now! Gnosticism teaches that, in actuality, Satan (who, in the Gnostic beliefs, is given the feminine name Sophia and worshiped as the "queen" of heaven) is good while the God of the Bible, the Creator of earth/matter, is evil because he has given mankind laws that limit our ability to do as we please. This teaching has been around for a long time. Check out the prophet Jeremiah's words in Jeremiah 7:17-20;24 and 44:15-17.

> "Do you not see what they are doing in the towns of Judah and in the streets of Jerusalem? The children gather wood, the fathers light the fire, and the women knead the dough and make cakes of bread

for the Queen of Heaven. They pour out drink offerings to other gods to provoke me to anger. But
am I the one they are provoking? declares the LORD.
Are they not rater harming themselves, to their own
shame? Therefore this is what the Sovereign LORD
says: My anger and my wrath will be poured out on
this place, on man and beast, on the trees of the field
and on the fruit of the ground, and it will burn and
not be quenched...But they did not listen or pay attention; instead, they followed the stubborn inclina-
tions of their evil hearts."

"Then all the men who knew that their wives were
burning incense to other gods, along with all the
women who were present – a large assembly – and
all the people living in Lower and Upper Egypt, said
to Jeremiah, 'We will not listen to the message you
have spoken to us in the name of the LORD! We will
certainly do everything we said we would: We will
burn incense to the Queen of Heaven and will pour
out drink offerings to her just as we and our father
and kings and our officials did in the towns of Judah
and in the streets of Jerusalem.'"

According to the Gnostics, God limits and restrains people
from being who they really are – gods who have the right to do as
they please and seek what they want. Pleasure is the goal, while
God, with his limiting laws and commands, is the problem. Thus,
according to Gnosticism, God is the one who is actually evil by
preventing us from doing as we please – enjoying sensuality and
life without borders or regulations. As pointed out, this belief
system is still alive and well today, heavily promoted by way of
the most influential realm on earth: entertainment media. When
stripped of all its layers, the essence of Gnosticism glorifies

Satan and beckons humanity to fulfill the lusts of the flesh. It is anti-Jesus, and rejects God. Be faithful to the Lord Jesus and hold on to the truth, doing his will to the end.

* **Revelation 2:26** → Those who say "no" to the world's pull (to compromise their spiritual and moral beliefs) and choose instead to say "yes" to the commands of God will rule and reign with Jesus forever. There is an eternal kingdom that exists, God's kingdom, and he will grant positions of authority to all who long for that kingdom of righteousness. The apostle Paul wrote to disciples of Jesus who were infants in the faith, caught up in trivial arguments and factions with each other, even taking each other to court before pagan judges. He wrote to remind them of their future as co-regents with the Lord Jesus of his eternal kingdom:

> If any of you has a dispute with another, dare he take it before the ungdly for judgment instead of before the saints (disciples of Jesus)? Do you not know that the saints will judge the world? And if you are to judge the world, are you not competent to judge trivial cases? Do you not know that we will judge angels? How much more the things of this life! [I Corinthians 6:1-3]

* **Revelation 2:27** → Millions of people flock to movies each year to see fictional heroes fight against evil for the purpose of upholding justice, truth, and righteousness. Movie-goers love it when those heroes use their incredible skills, powers, and weapons to trample the enemy so that good prevails over wickedness. Well, as this verse points out, Jesus will one day do in reality what these characters do in fiction – vanquish evil. Prior to Jesus establishing his never-ending kingdom on a radically transformed earth (see Revelation 21), he will come from heaven to make war against the rebellious nations on earth. We will

discuss when reviewing Revelation 19. A description of Jesus in this battle (referred to as Armageddon) is below:

> Who is this, robed in splendor, striding forward in the greatness of his strength? 'It is I, speaking in righteousness, mighty to save,' Why are your garments red, like those of one treading the winepress? 'I have trodden the winepress alone; from the nations no one was with me. I trampled them in my anger and trod them down in my wrath; their blood spattered my garments, and I stained all my clothing. For the day of vengeance was in my heart, and the year of my redemption has come. I looked, but there was no one to help, I was appalled that no one gave support; so my own arm worked salvation for me, and my own wrath sustained me. I trampled the nations in my anger; in my wrath I made them drunk and poured their blood on the ground.'" [Isaiah 63:1(b)-6]

* **Revelation 2:28-29** → Jesus is the morning star. What he most desires to give those who trust Him – love, peace, joy and purpose – matches the longings which burn so deeply within every human being. Ecclesiastes 3:11 says that in the heart of people are deep longings, like deep voids in their souls, that only God himself, their Creator, can fill. Think about this: on Christmas each year, millions of children open Christmas gifts to find electronic toys that run on batteries. Try as they might, without putting the proper batteries in the toys, their toys will not run. By way of this illustration, God himself is the "Battery" that will cause our lives to operate properly.

Chapter 9

First Love – Forsaken

Revelation 3:1-6

MUTANT INSIGHT

Wolverine: "What are you talking about? We're mutants; God gave up on us a long time ago."
Nightcrawler: "No my friend, God does not give up on his children – human or mutant. He is there for us in our times of joy and to help us when we are in pain, if we let him."
Wolverine: "Don't give me that easy-answer garbage! I've tried; don't you think I want that? I don't need a sermon from a circus-boy preacher!"
Nightcrawler: "We are alike, you and I. Angry at the world – and ourselves. My pain told me to seek God; yours tore you away. "

[X-Men The Animated Series: Nightcrawler]

Anger at God over expectations of what you thought he should have done in your life may have caused you to harden your heart toward Him. Perhaps you've been hurt by others or wanted to realize a dream and believe that God let you down. You feel as though he didn't listen to your prayers and didn't care about your situation. So you've decided that you won't care about him. Friend, don't allow your pain – whether caused by others or your expectations – prevent you from experiencing God's healing. The ramifications of sin impact us in different ways that result in real hurt and pain. This is what God warned Adam and Eve about.

Their actions still impact us today. God's love is greater. Surrender, trust, and let him heal you.

Wake Up!

Revelation 3:1-6

> [1] *To the angel of the church in Sardis write: These are the words of him who holds the seven spirits of God and the seven stars. I know your deeds; you have a reputation of being alive, but you are dead.* [2] *Wake up! Strengthen what remains and is about to die, for I have not found your deeds complete in the sight of my God.* [3] *Remember, therefore, what you have received and heard; obey it, and repent. But if you do not wake up, I will come like a thief, and you will not know at what time I will come to you.* [4] *Yet you have a few people in Sardis who have not soiled their clothes. They will walk with me, dressed in white, for they are worthy.* [5] *He who overcomes will, like them, be dressed in white. I will never blot out his name from the book of life, but will acknowledge his name before my Father and his angels.* [6] *He who has an ear, let him hear what the Spirit says to the churches.*

* **Revelation 3:1-2** → Sardis was an important city during both the Persian and Roman empires. "It was a natural fortress city, built on a plateau having unscalable cliff walls on three sides. It was the center for the production of Electrum, a gold and silver alloy used in the plating of pagan statues and idols. It was also the center for a thriving carpet and wool industry, and the first coins in Asia Minor were minted here."[3]

Unfortunately, Sardis had acquired a reputation for compromised moral standards, to which Jesus was speaking when he referenced their deadness. Spiritual deadness refers to their outward appearance of being about the things of God, while actuality, their hearts, motives, and secret actions were not reflective of God at all. Jesus warned this church to wake up and strengthen what was about to die.

Jesus could offer the same warning to many of us today. Neither spiritual pride nor spiritual apathy are pleasing in his sight. His statement "...for I have not found your deeds complete in the sight of my God [the Father]" does not suggest that our good deeds or works lead to salvation. No good deeds or sacrificial works can make us holy or qualify us for heaven. Only the work of Christ on the cross can provide forgiveness of sins and salvation of one's soul [read Ephesians 2:8-9]. The deeds referenced in this verse are specific works that those already devoted to Jesus have been called to carry out in his name. But because of their spiritual deadness, the believers in Sardis had never completed their appointed tasks.

* **Revelation 3:3** → Jesus expects those whom he has redeemed from the power and penalty of sin to obey his word and carry out his will, employing all the gifts and talents He has given them to fulfill his purposes [see Matthew 25:14-30]. If God's children continue to walk in disobedience, God has made it clear that He is not slow to discipline, just as loving parents discipline their children. The goal of this parental discipline is to raise up children who walk in obedience, represent the family name well, and be all that they should be. Consider these words:

> And have you completely forgotten this word of
> encouragement that addresses you as a father ad-
> dresses his son? It says, "My son, do not make light

of the Lord's discipline, and do not lose heart when he rebukes you, because the Lord disciplines the one he loves, and he chastens everyone he accepts as his son." Endure hardship as discipline; God is treating you as his children. For what children are not disciplined by their father? If you are not disciplined—and everyone undergoes discipline—then you are not legitimate, not true sons and daughters at all. Moreover, we have all had human fathers who disciplined us and we respected them for it. How much more should we submit to the Father of spirits and live! They disciplined us for a little while as they thought best; but God disciplines us for our good, in order that we may share in his holiness. No discipline seems pleasant at the time, but painful. Later on, however, it produces a harvest of righteousness and peace for those who have been trained by it. Therefore, strengthen your feeble arms and weak knees. "Make level paths for your feet," so that the lame may not be disabled, but rather healed. [Hebrews 12:5-13]

MUTANT INSIGHT

Wolverine: "Just have a little faith pal; I hear it can work wonders."

[X-Men The Animated Series: Bloodlines]

Even the most hardened person, if they will dare to surrender their hearts and minds to God's love, will discover that even a little faith in God can move mountains [see Luke 17:5-6]. You may say, "You don't know me. I'm not a person of faith." Well,

I would disagree. You are most definitely a person who walks by faith every day. For example, every time you eat food prepared at restaurants, fly on planes, and ride on elevators, you are displaying great faith in people – people you don't even know and probably have never met. Exercise that faith toward God and watch your life change forever!

---

    * **Revelation 3:4** → While the majority of people in Sardis were not devoted followers of Jesus, there were a few people who were. Jesus' statement about them not having soiled their clothes means that these particular believers were not living in corruption and moral filth like other citizens of Sardis. The Bible uses the metaphor that those with clean clothes (white linen) are those whose souls have been cleansed by the blood of the Lamb (Jesus) and who live righteously for him [Revelation 19:7,14].

    This truth is contrasted with the vile and wicked practices common in Sardis to the worship of the Greek goddess Cybele. According to Greek mythology, Cybele was initially a hermaphroditic (male and female) demon named Agdistis – supposedly produced from Zeus' semen that fell to earth. Bizarre, right? Here's how Greek mythology describes Cybele:

> The other gods were afraid of Agdistis and severed its male sex organ, which fell to the earth and grew into an almond tree. After this, Agdistis became the female goddess Cybele. Later, Cybele fell in love with her son/grandson, Attis, and took him in as a lover. One day, in a fit of jealousy, she drove him mad and he castrated himself and died, but was resurrected as a pine tree. In response to these legends, the people of Sardis worshiped Cybele and held almond and pine trees in reverence, while also hold-

ing fertility festivals in celebration of Attis' rebirth. In these celebrations, all the people of Sardis would wear white robes, and the worshipers and priests of Cybele (called 'galli') would parade down the main street of Sardis, cutting themselves in ecstasy until they reached the shrine of Cybele (later integrated into the temple of Artemis in the third century B.C.), where a few of the worshipers would castrate themselves and offer their severed parts to Cybele. Those along the parade route (or within the parade, itself) who had the blood of the worshipers sprayed upon their cloaks were said to be favored by the goddess.[4]

This helps clarify what Jesus was referring to when he mentioned the soiling of clothes by those in the Sardis church. Many of them had fallen into the wicked practices popular in the city, participating in the Satan-inspired "worship parties" that were a part of that culture. The word of commendation that Jesus gives in this verse is to his faithful followers who refused to compromise worship of God for the worship of idols and, subsequently, demons.

    * **Revelation 3:5-6** → Decisions must be made daily to either obey or reject the Lord and his will for us. His promise to his devoted followers within the church of Sardis who overcame pressures to yield to wrongdoing applies to modern-day followers of Christ. Jesus promises eternal life to all who yield to his lordship, a yielding that is demonstrated by their transformed lives and obedience to righteousness. The Book of Life to which Jesus refers in Revelation 3:5 is also called the Lamb's Book of Life in Revelation 13:8 and 21:27. During his earthly ministry, Jesus made a similar promise to his early disciples that one day he would acknowledge his faithful followers before God the Father and the angels:

Whoever acknowledges me before others, I will also acknowledge before my Father in heaven. But whoever disowns me before others, I will disown before my Father in heaven. [Matthew 10:32,33]

Chapter 10

The Open Door Is Closing...Get In!

Revelation 3:7-22

Wolverine: "Don't tell me about God. What kind of God would allow men to do this to me (shows claws)?"
Nightcrawler: "Our ability to understand God's purposes is limited. But we take comfort in the fact that his love is limitless."

[X-Men The Animated Series: Nightcrawler]

E ven Wolverine, with his limitless physical healing powers, can't escape the enduring pain of emotional and spiritual wounds. Nightcrawler, who is no stranger to rejection and pain, tells Wolverine that he needs to go to God for healing and restoration. This speaks to the profound truth that directly addresses the proverbial "hole in the heart" to which people often refer (as in, there's something missing on the inside – even after success, fame, and fortune come) as expressed in Ecclesiastes 3:11,

> He [God] has made everything beautiful in its time.
> He has also set eternity in the human heart; yet no
> one can fathom what God has done from beginning
> to end.

The key words in the above verse are, "He has also set eternity in the human heart". What this means is that within every person there is a spiritual vacuum of meaning and purpose that can only be filled by God's abiding presence and love. That is why no pursuit of fame, riches, or pleasure will ever truly satisfy the human soul, a reality often seen played out so tragically in the lives of many so-called "successful" people.

All people bring pain into their own lives due to poor choices. But some of us have also had to endure great pain that has come by the hands of others. God will judge all non-repentant people for heinous acts of sin and self-absorbed evil. However, it is important to guard against Satan's deception; don't allow bitterness and anger to push you away from God's love and into a place of poor decision-making and judgment – whether by authorities in this life or by God in the eternal life to come.

Brotherly Love is Great, But Gods Love Is Better

Revelation 3:7-13

> *[7] To the angel of the church in Philadelphia write: These are the words of him who is holy and true, who holds the key of David. What he opens no one can shut, and what he shuts no one can open. [8] I know your deeds. See, I have placed before you an open door that no one can shut. I know that you have little strength, yet you have kept my word and have not denied my name. [9] I will make those who are of the synagogue of Satan, who claim to be Jews though they are not, but are liars—I will make them come and fall down at your feet and acknowledge that I have loved you. [10] Since you have kept my command to endure patiently, I will also keep you from the hour of trial that is*

going to come upon the whole world to test those who live on the earth. [11] I am coming soon. Hold on to what you have, so that no one will take your crown. [12] Him who overcomes I will make a pillar in the temple of my God. Never again will he leave it. I will write on him the name of my God and the name of the city of my God, the new Jerusalem, which is coming down out of heaven from my God; and I will also write on him my new name. [13] He who has an ear, let him hear what the Spirit says to the churches.

* Revelation 3:7 → Philadelphia was located in the region of modern day Alasheir (in Turkey). The name Philadelphia means "brotherly love". The Scriptures foretold that the coming Messiah (Christ) would be a direct descendant of King David. David is lauded by the Jews as their most decorated and celebrated king. Jesus, whom David will serve [read Acts 2:25-36], is *the* King of all other kings and holds all power. He holds the keys to the kingdom of Israel, all the earth, and the entire universe. Important to note is that, of the seven churches addressed in Revelation 2 and 3, Philadelphia—along with Smyrna—received no words of condemnation from Jesus. This church had sound doctrine *and* lived right. Without love, doctrine (principles, or truth) leads to legalism and sterile relationships. Without doctrine, love leads to humanism and chaos.

* Revelation 3:8 → Okay, pause for a moment and think about this: Jesus knows all of your deeds, both those done openly and the ones done in secret. Furthermore, he knows your motives, thoughts, and words even before you think or act on them. He is perfect and hates sin. Thus, based on what he knows about people, He should reject them because of their sin and rebellion. However, the open door he places before each individual person is the door of relationship with Him. To have a relationship with the living God of the universe is the most fulfilling attainment one can ever achieve. Do as the Philadelphians; keep God's Word and do not deny the name of Jesus.

* **Revelation 3:9** → The synagogue of Satan was discussed in our reading of Revelation 2:9. Like Smyrna, the city of Philadelphia also had a large Jewish population that was very hostile towards Christians. The Jewish synagogue was referred to as the "synagogue of Satan" because they were not spiritually of God's family [see Romans 2:17-29], but belonged to Satan [see John 8:42-47]. The city itself was devoted to Roman emperor worship which made it dangerous for believers in Jesus to be open about their faith.

* **Revelation 3:10** → For all who place their allegiance, hope and their very lives by faith in the Lord Jesus Christ, he promises forgiveness of the penalty of sin (eternal damnation) and a position of security and permanence in God's eternal kingdom. This verse speaks to all Christians who will be alive during the last days, prior to the coming of the Antichrist and the beginning of the seven-year period referred to in the Bible as the Tribulation. During this period of time, God will pour out his judgment on the earth. This horrific period of time is referenced in subsequent chapters in Revelation.

* **Revelation 3:11-13** → Jesus commended the church at Philadelphia for living with purpose and glorifying the Lord. In light of his impending second coming, he admonishes His followers today to do the same. His promises to all overcomers of filthy living and wickedness include heavenly rewards and eternally secure positions in his never-ending and perfect kingdom. Faithful followers of Christ, who have been reborn by his Spirit, will be marked with the holy inscribed names of God the Father, God the Son, and the spectacular New Jerusalem that we'll read about in chapter twenty-one.

MUTANT INSIGHT

Wolverine: "Hmmm, I used to buy into all of that [talk about God's love]. But I've lived too long and I've done too much."
Nightcrawler: "Life will always be hard. I understand this better than most. Yet despite it all, people of every faith believe that there is a God who loves them. Can so many be wrong? Open your heart Herr Logan. Would it hurt so much to see the world through different eyes?"

[X-Men The Animated Series: Nightcrawler]

Wolverine's pain due to the wrongdoings of others against him has caused doubts to arise in his mind about God. Furthermore, the acknowledgement of his own sin makes him think that he is not worthy of God's love, forgiveness, and restoration. Nightcrawler affirms that this life can be tough. However, he also testifies that God's existence and beckoning to all people is real. How about stepping up to Nightcrawler's challenge to Wolverine? Try looking at the world, even your own life, through the lenses of faith and obedience to God.

Lukewarm Commitment Is Rejected

Revelation 3:14-22

[14] To the angel of the church in Laodicea write: These are the words of the Amen, the faithful and true witness, the ruler of God's creation. [15] I

know your deeds, that you are neither cold nor hot. I wish you were either one or the other! [16] *So, because you are lukewarm—neither hot nor cold—I am about to spit you out of my mouth.* [17] *You say, 'I am rich; I have acquired wealth and do not need a thing.' But you do not realize that you are wretched, pitiful, poor, blind and naked.* [18] *I counsel you to buy from me gold refined in the fire, so you can become rich; and white clothes to wear, so you can cover your shameful nakedness; and salve to put on your eyes, so you can see.* [19] *Those whom I love I rebuke and discipline. So be earnest, and repent.* [20] *Here I am! I stand at the door and knock. If anyone hears my voice and opens the door, I will come in and eat with him, and he with me.* [21] *To him who overcomes, I will give the right to sit with me on my throne, just as I overcame and sat down with my Father on his throne.* [22] *He who has an ear, let him hear what the Spirit says to the churches.*

* **Revelation 3:14** → Did you know that the word "amen" has two meanings based on who says it. When the Lord says it, the word means "it is and shall be so". When people say it, it means "so be it" or "so let it be". In this verse, Jesus reveals again who He is – the ruler of God's creation and the final Authority.

* **Revelation 3:15-16** → Jesus makes it clear that indifference towards Him (being lukewarm) is unacceptable and will result in doom for all who reject him. Lukewarm individuals (and churches they make up) are characterized by indifference, compromise, toleration of evil, and/or accepting views of others that are in opposition to the Scriptures. Jesus says that he will vomit (forcefully spew away) from his presence all who are actively against him. Lukewarm people, according to Jesus, are not for him.

* **Revelation 3:17-19** → Laodicea is present day Pamukkale (in modern day Turkey). It was a wealthy city and known for its banking system, medical school, and textile industry. Jesus addresses these three areas of pride in his statement to the church in this verse. He said to those who boasted of their financial system, medicine, and production of fine clothing were, in fact, spiritually poor, blind, and naked. This same warning could be given to many today. If you fall in this category, take heart and repent.

* **Revelation 3:20-22** → The concluding scene of each episode in the cartoon series "The Flintstones" shows Fred Flintstone being locked outside of his own home by one of his pet animals. Each episode ended with this scene, with Fred yelling out his wife's name "Wilma!", asking her to let him back into his own house. In Revelation 3:20-22, the Lord Jesus is seen knocking on the hearts of wayward Christians, asking them if they are willing to open the door of their stubborn hearts and let Him have entrance. If you need to repent and let the King of glory have access to previously closed doors in your life (desires, emotions, feelings, and mind), do so today! Overcomers will rule and reign with Christ the King. Do you have an ear to hear?

Chapter 11

Throne of No Games

Revelation 4:1-5

MUTANT INSIGHT

Wolverine: "I will give thanks to you O' Lord. For though you were angry with me, your anger turned away and you comforted me. I will trust and not be afraid."

[X-Men The Animated Series: Nightcrawler]

Wolverine's words above are actually a direct quote from the Bible. They were originally stated by the prophet Isaiah [check out Isaiah 12:1-2]. Have you ever thanked God for his mercy toward you – not treating you as your sins deserve?

God commands us to analyze where we are in life and, if need be, acknowledge our sin, confess it to him, turn away from rebellious living, and allow him to transform us. Many people appear to walk confidently with an outward swagger, yet on the inside they are very weak and afraid. God is greater than everyone and everything, including any anxiety, enemy, and self-defeating ego that weigh people down. Surrender today and trust God. He will not disappoint you.

The Open Door and The Emerald Rainbow

Revelation 4:1-5

> [1] *After this I looked, and there before me was a door standing open in heaven. And the voice I had first heard speaking to me like a trumpet said, "Come up here, and I will show you what must take place after this."* [2] *At once I was in the Spirit, and there before me was a throne in heaven with someone sitting on it.* [3] *And the one who sat there had the appearance of jasper and carnelian. A rainbow, resembling an emerald, encircled the throne.* [4] *Surrounding the throne were twenty-four other thrones, and seated on them were twenty-four elders. They were dressed in white and had crowns of gold on their heads.* [5] *From the throne came flashes of lightning, rumblings and peals of thunder. Before the throne, seven lamps were blazing. These are the seven spirits of God.*

* **Revelation 4:1** → Revelation 4 (along with Revelation 5) is an introduction to chapters 6-20. The open door that John saw in heaven refers to the fact that God is allowing sinners to enter his kingdom—by way of the sacrificial death of the Lord Jesus Christ. Jesus' statement to John, "Come up here, and I will show you what must take place after this", has a two-part meaning. First, it was a command for John to go where Jesus was (heaven) in order to receive the rest of the revelation of what God's plan is for the future [see Revelation 1:1]. Second, it points to an event that all true believers of Jesus Christ will one day experience—a day on which they will be supernaturally and instantaneously translated from earth to heaven, to be gathered together with

Jesus in heaven just prior to when God pours out his judgment on the world due to man's rebellion.

The "church age" is the period of time spanning from Jesus' ascension into heaven after his resurrection to this day in history, referred to as the rapture of the church. The word "rapture", used in the context of end-time events described in the Bible, is derived from the Latin word *rapturo*, which is a translation of the Greek verb "caught up" or "snatch away" that's found in the Bible (remember, the original writing of the New Testament was in Greek).

> According to the Lord's word, we tell you that we who are still alive, who are left until the coming of the Lord, will certainly not precede those who have fallen asleep. For the Lord himself will come down from heaven, with a loud command, with the voice of the archangel and with the trumpet call of God, and the dead in Christ will rise first. After that, we who are still alive and are left will be *caught up* together with them in the clouds to meet the Lord in the air. And so we will be with the Lord forever. [I Thessalonians 4:15-17]

Think of a rescue worker who is responding to an emergency call indicating that a baby is inside of a house that's on fire. What will the rescue-worker do first? Will he wait until the flames are completely extinguished and then look for the baby OR will he attempt to pull out the baby from the burning house as soon as possible, before total destruction of the house occurs? Any rescue worker worth their salt would attempt to rescue the baby first. Similarly, just before God's final judgment on the world because of sin (events spelled out in Revelation 6-18), there will be a pulling out, or "snatching away" (rapture) from the world of all those who belong to Jesus.

The last church mentioned in Revelation 3 is Laodicea. Its spiritual state, characterized as being "lukewarm" (indifferent), is indicative of the state of many people who today profess Jesus as Savior. If that is you, make a U-turn in your desires, thinking, words and actions.

For the first three chapters of the Apocalypse (Revelation), the focus has been Jesus and the Church (his disciples). Beginning with Chapter 4, however, the church is not mentioned again until Revelation 19, when Jesus returns to earth in fulfillment of the words of this prophecy.

Why the abrupt change of focus? Because the Church (all true followers of Christ) will be translated to heaven (raptured) to escape the future period referred to as the Tribulation/Great Tribulation on the earth. The Church is referenced and discussed consistently in the first three chapters of Revelation. However, beginning with chapter four and verse one, it is not mentioned again (not one time) until chapter nineteen – when Jesus returns to the earth. Why is the Church not mentioned? Because all true believers in Jesus will be raptured (taken out of the world) just prior to the Tribulation and Great Tribulation years.

This will be a period of time in which God's judgment will be poured out on the earth because of mankind's wickedness. During this time, the overwhelming majority of the world's population will be anti-God and will follow the man whom the Bible refers to as the Antichrist.

* **Revelation 4:2-3** → John was immediately translated to heaven where he beheld a glorious throne. The one seated on this majestic throne was sparkling and dazzling to behold in his indescribable glory, power, and majesty. The words John uses to describe him are words used to describe precious and semi-precious stones. Both jasper and ruby are transparent, fiery red precious stones. They are used figuratively in these verses to describe the One whom John sees seated on the throne. But these two stones are actually first mentioned in the Old Testament, in the context of the breastpiece that God commanded Moses to have made for his brother Aaron (and Aaron's sons) to wear as priests.

This breastpiece, about nine inches long and nine inches wide, was worn over the chest and heart of the high priest (Aaron). It had four rows precious stones with each row having three stones, totaling twelve. Yes, this might certainly remind you of the fictitious breastplate that Tony Stark (Iron Man) created to guard his heart. Not to mention the powerful infinity stones that are in the comics. The Bible is so awesome! That's where many writers of comics and movies get their material – from the Author of all authors. For all you comic book and movie fans, think about the fictitious Infiniti Gauntlet as you read this description of the high-priests' breast-piece:

> [God speaking to Moses] Fashion a breastpiece for making decisions – the work of a skilled craftsman. Make it like the ephod: of gold, and of blue, purple and scarlet yarn, and of finely twisted linen. It is to be square – a span long and a span wide – and fold-ed double. Then mount four rows of precious stones on it. The first row shall be carnelian, chrysolite and beryl; the second row shall be turquoise, lapis lazuli and emerald; the third row shall be jacinth, agate and amethyst; the fourth row shall be topaz, onyx and jasper. Mount them in gold filigree settings. There are to be twelve stones, one for each of the names of the sons of Israel, each engraved like a seal with the name of one of the twelve tribes. [Exodus 28:15-21]

The first stone on the breastpiece was the carnelian (ruby) and the twelfth was the jasper. The first stone had the name of Jacob's (Israel's) first-born son, Reuben, engraved on it. The twelfth stone had the name of the last-born, Benjamin, engraved on it. However, John's description of the one sitting on the throne begins first with jasper (Benjamin) and then follows with carnelian (Reuben). The name Reuben means, "behold the son". It points to Jesus' first coming as the son who was offered by God the Father as the sacrificial Lamb to pay the penalty for mankind's sins. The name Benjamin means "the son of my right hand" or "the son of my power". It points to Jesus' second coming as the royal King of kings and Lord of lords. The description of the enthroned one as sitting indicates that his work as Redeemer is complete.

Did you know that God created the multi-colored rainbow that we see in the sky as a visible sign of his covenant with man to never again destroy the world with a flood? He made this covenant after He destroyed the world during the time of Noah as judgment against the excessive vileness of mankind [see Genesis 9:8-17]. The rainbow that John sees circling the throne in heaven resembles emerald (green). The color green falls in the center of the sequence of colors found in rainbows (red, orange, yellow, green, blue, indigo, and violet). Why green? Perhaps because green is the color most commonly associated with life, nature, and growth. "In surveys made in Europe and the United States, green is the color most commonly associated with nature, youth, spring, hope, and envy."[5] "Green is also the traditional color of safety and permission; a green light means go ahead, a green card permits permanent residence in the United States."[6] The emerald stone on the breastpiece had the name "Judah" engraved on it and means "praise". God the Son, the Lord Jesus Christ, is the life-giver of all things and worthy of all praise:

> For in him all things were created: things in heaven
> and on earth, visible and invisible, whether thrones
> or powers or rulers or authorities; all things have

been created through him and for him. He is before all things, and in him all things hold together. And he is the head of the body, the church; he is the beginning and the firstborn from among the dead, so that in everything he might have the supremacy. [Colossians 1:16-18]

MUTANT INSIGHT

Magneto: "Where were you when my father and mother were slaughtered in this place?"
Apocalypse: "Asleep. Trapped in darkness. I was not there for you my son. But I am here now...Everything they've built will fall. And from the ashes of their world, we'll build a better one!"

[X-Men: Apocalypse]

Having just seen his wife and daughter murdered and been told by Apocalypse that he is deity, Magneto asks the question above when Apocalypse transports him to Auschwitz, where his parents were exterminated during World War II. His question is rooted in sincerity, deep pain, and a desire to be set free from the downward spirals of anger and bitterness. Apocalypse's reply is one to be expected from a deity-pretender. He is neither omniscient (all-knowing) nor omnipotent (all-powerful); thus, when asked the question by Magneto, he admits that he was in a deep sleep when Magneto's parents were murdered – trapped and unable to rescue them even if he wanted to.

In life, the pain of loss can be as real as that which Magneto was undergoing. God, however, has never slept, never been trapped, and knows all things past, present, and future. We can lift our prayers to him. He cares for us when we go through the valley of darkness and loss, hoping that we will trust him for peace, renewal of hope, and joyous future.

---

* Revelation 4:4 → The twenty-four elders are a combination of two groups. The first group consists of the twelve sons of Jacob (whom God gave the name Israel), from which the twelve tribes of Israel descended. The second group includes the original eleven disciples (excluding Judas Iscariot, who betrayed Jesus) plus the apostle Paul, who were all appointed by Jesus to be his apostles. In Matthew 19:28, while speaking to the original twelve disciples,

> Jesus said to them, 'Truly I tell you, at the renewal of all things, when the Son of Man sits on his glorious throne, you who have followed me will also sit on twelve thrones, judging the twelve tribes of Israel.'

Approximately thirty years before John received the vision and words of the book of Revelation, the apostle Paul wrote the following to the Ephesian church about being unified in love and purpose:

> So then you are no longer strangers and aliens, but you are fellow citizens with the saints, and are of God's household, having been built on the foundation of the apostles and prophets, Christ Jesus Himself being the corner stone, in whom the whole building, being fitted together, is growing into a holy temple in the Lord, in whom you also are being built together into a dwelling of God in the Spirit. [Ephesians 2:19-21]

When we begin our review of chapter twenty-one of the Apocalypse (Revelation) of Jesus Christ, we will read about the future heavenly city, called the New Jerusalem, which will come down to earth from heaven. It will have twelve high gates, with each one inscribed with one of the names of the twelve tribes of Israel. The great city will also have twelve foundation stones, with each stone having the inscription of one of the names of the twelve apostles:

> And he carried me away in the Spirit to a mountain great and high, and showed me the holy city, Jerusalem, coming down out of heaven from God, having the glory of God. Her brilliance was like a very costly stone, as a stone of crystal-clear jasper. It had a great and high wall, with twelve gates, and at the gates twelve angels; and names were written on them, which are the names of the twelve tribes of the sons of Israel. There were three gates on the east and three gates on the north and three gates on the south and three gates on the west. And the wall of the city had twelve foundation stones, and on them were the twelve names of the twelve apostles of the Lamb. [Revelation 21:10-14]

* **Revelation 4:5** → God is beyond our comprehension in power, majesty, and holiness. He is the God of love, mercy and grace to all who surrender to his authority and perfect rule. However, to those who refuse his Lordship, he is a consuming fire and dreadful judge. Check out what Hebrews 10:26-27,31 have to say:

> If we deliberately keep on sinning after we have received the knowledge of the truth, no sacrifice for sins is left, but only a fearful expectation of judg-

ment and of raging fire that will consume the enemies of God...It is a dreadful thing to fall into the
hands of the living God.

See, my friends, the world has been duped. Satan has done a
masterful job of portraying Jesus as being just a "nice guy" and
a pushover. The devil has perpetuated a belief system among
the masses that cause them to believe that they can do whatever
they want to do and "good ol' Jesus will say, 'Well, I was hoping
you'd do better, but it doesn't matter...I wasn't expecting too
much from you all anyway'." Not!

The seven spirits (lamps) before the throne represent the
seven-fold aspects of the Spirit of God:

> The Spirit of the LORD [the Spirit of *holiness/righ-
> teousness*] will rest on him – the Spirit of *wisdom*
> and of *understanding*, the Spirit of *counsel* and of
> *might*, the Spirit of the *knowledge* and *fear* of the
> LORD [Isaiah 11:2]

Chapter 12

Winged Creatures and a Sea of Glass

Revelation 4:6-11

Apocalypse: "Tiny meddling insects. They don't realize that he who controls time controls every eventual reality!"

[X-Men The Animated Series: Beyond Good and Evil, Part 3]

In his quest for immortality and world domination, Apocalypse comes to understand that his limited abilities, being bound to time and space, are preventing him from accomplishing his goals—thus his desire to control time. On the contrary, God is before time itself. He created it, controls it, and is sovereign over all that happens – past, present, and future. The lyrics, "He's got the whole world in his hands…" are true. Submit to his love and lordship.

Four Living Creatures

Revelation 4:6-11

> ⁶ *Also before the throne there was what looked like a sea of glass, clear as crystal. In the center, around the throne, were four living creatures,*

and they were covered with eyes, in front and in back. [7] The first living creature was like a lion, the second was like an ox, the third had a face like a man, the fourth was like a flying eagle. [8] Each of the four living creatures had six wings and was covered with eyes all around, even under his wings. Day and night they never stop saying: "Holy, holy, holy is the Lord God Almighty, who was, and is, and is to come." [9] Whenever the living creatures give glory, honor and thanks to him who sits on the throne and who lives for ever and ever, [10] the twenty-four elders fall down before him who sits on the throne, and worship him who lives for ever and ever. They lay their crowns before the throne and say: [11] "You are worthy, our Lord and God, to receive glory and honor and power, for you created all things, and by your will they were created and have their being."

* **Revelation 4:6-11** → God has created beings, both in this temporal world and the eternal one, that humans know nothing about. For example, there are species of fish and other sea creatures that have never even been seen because they live at depths beneath the sea far beyond man's ability to search. Likewise, there are heavenly beings such as these four living creatures in Revelation 4:6-11 that God has created for his eternal purposes, whose form and power can't be fathomed by humans. These creatures are referred to earlier in the Bible as seraphim ("seraph" is singular, "seraphim" is plural). The word means "burning ones". About 890 years before John's vision of Revelation, the prophet Isaiah had a similar vision of God on his throne with the seraphim flying above him:

In the year that King Uzziah died, I saw the Lord, high and exalted, seated on a throne; and the train of his robe filled the temple. Above him were seraphim, each with six wings: With two wings they covered their faces, with two they covered their feet, and with two they were flying. And they were calling to one another: 'Holy, holy, holy is the LORD Almighty; the whole earth is full of his glory.' At the sound of their voices the doorposts and thresholds shook and the temple was filled with smoke. [Isaiah 6:1-4]

Seraphim are different than cherubim (singular is cherub), another type of heavenly being with wings referred to in the Bible. Over the years, cherubs have been depicted as pudgy baby-like beings (think of fictitious Cupid with his arrow). However, this is not a true biblical characterization of them. The first mention of them is in Genesis, after Adam and Eve were deceived by Satan:

So the LORD God banished him from the Garden of Eden to work the ground from which he had been taken. After he drove the man out, he placed on the east side of the Garden of Eden cherubim and a flaming sword flashing back and forth to guard the way to the tree of life. [Genesis 3:23-24]

The other reference to cherubim in the Bible is given by the prophet Ezekiel:

I looked, and I saw a windstorm coming out of the north—an immense cloud with flashing lightning and surrounded by brilliant light. The center of the fire looked like glowing metal, and in the fire was what looked like four living creatures. In appearance their form was human, but each of them had four faces and four wings. Their legs were straight; their feet were like those of a calf and gleamed like burnished bronze. Under their wings on their four sides they had human hands. All four of them had faces and wings, and the wings of one touched the wings of another. Each one went straight ahead; they did not turn as they moved. Their faces looked like this: Each of the four had the face of a human being, and on the right side each had the face of a lion, and on the left the face of an ox; each also had the face of an eagle. Such were their faces. They each had two wings spreading out upward, each wing touching that of the creature on either side; and each had two other wings covering its body. Each one went straight ahead. Wherever the spirit would go, they would go, without turning as they went. The appearance of the living creatures was like burning coals of fire or like torches. Fire moved back and forth among the creatures; it was bright, and lightning flashed out of it. The creatures sped back and forth like flashes of lightning. [Ezekiel 1:4-14]

Cherubim are also described in the construction of the Ark of the Covenant (yes, the one depicted in the Indiana Jones film, "Raiders of the Lost Ark"). The ark was God's earthly "dwelling place" where his Spirit resided among the Israelites during their exodus from enslavement in Egypt. The ark was a wooden chest covered with gold. Sculptures of the cherubim were placed on the lid of the ark according to God's command to Moses:

And make two cherubim out of hammered gold at the ends of the cover. Make one cherub on one end and the second cherub on the other; make the cherubim of one piece with the cover, at the two ends. The cherubim are to have their wings spread upward, overshadowing the cover with them. The cherubim are to face each other, looking toward the cover. [Exodus 25:18-20]

So now you know the truth: seraphim and cherubim have wings, but angels do not. Yes, I know, all your life you've seen angels depicted with wings. But this is biblically inaccurate.

Chapter 13

The Lamb Is Worthy!

Revelation 5:1-14

Apocalypse: "You are only delaying the inevitable. I, who am eternal, can never be defeated."

[X-Men The Animated Series: Time Fugitives, Part 1]

Like the fictional character Apocalypse, many people throughout time have been duped in their thinking to actually believe that they are the kings and queens of their destiny. They have never seriously contemplated life after death and their inevitable one-on-one future meeting (judgment) with the Lord Jesus Christ. He is the eternal One to whom all must one day give an account. The *X-Men: Apocalypse* movie has the tagline, "Only the Strong Will Survive". In reality, when it comes to our lives and eternal fate, Jesus the Savior's tagline is, "Only the Saved Will Survive".

Fierce as a Lion, Gentle as a Lamb

Revelation 5:1-6

¹ Then I saw in the right hand of him who sat on the throne a scroll with writing on both sides and sealed with seven seals. ² And I saw a mighty angel proclaiming in a loud voice, "Who is worthy to break the seals and open the scroll?" ³ But no one in heaven or on earth or under the earth could open the scroll or even look inside it. ⁴ I wept and wept because no one was found who was worthy to open the scroll or look inside. ⁵ Then one of the elders said to me, "Do not weep! See, the Lion of the tribe of Judah, the Root of David, has triumphed. He is able to open the scroll and its seven seals." ⁶ Then I saw a Lamb, looking as if it had been slain, standing in the center of the throne, encircled by the four living creatures and the elders. He had seven horns and seven eyes, which are the seven spirits of God sent out into all the earth.

* **Revelation 5:1** → John sees both God the Father, who is holding a sealed scroll, and a mighty angel. The angel's appearance and voice alone, without any physical demonstration of power, convinced John that this being was mighty. It's like what comes to mind when one sees the average cover of superhero comic books. The depictions of these characters are always in dynamic scenes that reveal their power and presence. The angel's question, "Who is worthy...?", pertains to who has power and authority to break the seals and open the scroll.

* **Revelation 5:3-6** → In these verses Jesus is referred to as the Lion of the tribe of Judah, The Root of David, and the Lamb of God. Lions are referred to in the animal kingdom as the "king of the jungle". These verses remind us that he is not merely a man. Rather, he is the incarnate God who will come to earth a second time as the conquering King. He is the King of kings and King of creation.

Jesus is also referred to as the Root of David because before King David was born, reigned and died, Jesus existed in eternity past. He is not only a descendant of David as pertaining to his humanity, but he also existed before David, being divine and eternal.

Thirdly, Jesus is referred to as a Lamb because he came to earth about two thousand years ago for one purpose: to die a sacrificial death for mankind and provide salvation (the forgiveness of sins) for all who believe. The seven horns speak to his power and dominion over the nations of the earth. The number seven is used hundreds of times in the Bible. In both the physical and spiritual dimensions, it is the number of completeness and perfection.

A Heavenly Choir

Revelation 5:7-14

> [7] *He came and took the scroll from the right hand of him who sat on the throne.* [8] *And when he had taken it, the four living creatures and the twenty-four elders fell down before the Lamb. Each one had a harp and they were holding golden bowls full of incense, which are the prayers of the saints.* [9] *And they sang a new song: "You are worthy to take the scroll and to open its seals, because you were slain, and with your blood you purchased men for God from every tribe and lan-*

guage and people and nation. [10] You have made them to be a kingdom and priests to serve our God, and they will reign on the earth." [11] Then I looked and heard the voice of many angels, numbering thousands upon thousands, and ten thousand times ten thousand. They encircled the throne and the living creatures and the elders. [12] In a loud voice they sang: "Worthy is the Lamb, who was slain, to receive power and wealth and wisdom and strength and honor and glory and praise!" [13] Then I heard every creature in heaven and on earth and under the earth and on the sea, and all that is in them, singing: "To him who sits on the throne and to the Lamb be praise and honor and glory and power, for ever and ever!" [14] The four living creatures said, "Amen," and the elders fell down and worshiped.

* **Revelation 5:7-14** → These verses reveal that Jesus is worthy to open the scroll—the title deed to the earth—because he willingly offered himself as the sacrifice for mankind's sins in order to ransom people (who place their trust in him) from the penalty and consequences of sin, which is eternal separation from God in hell. In his grace and mercy, Jesus not only ransom's sinners by His sacrificial death, but he goes further to guarantee that they will reign on the new earth with him forever. His future kingdom will be one of perfection, power, purity and peace.

Chapter 14

Horses, Horsemen and Death

Revelation 6:1-8

Apocalypse: "Each generation has cried out for a new world, but has built the same old one – corrupt and weak. But the new world shall come to pass. I will purge the earth of these benighted humans. Take the food from their mouths ...Turn their weapons against them...Exterminate them!"

[X-Men The Animated Series: Come the Apocalypse]

D aily news headlines confirm that there is mass corruption, violence, and chaos in the world. Many today long for a new world order, one that will bring about greater levels of peace and equity among people around the globe. This is a noble thought, but as long as sinful people sit in power, there will only be lopsided levels and temporary glimmers of peace in the world. Apocalypse's reference above to purging the earth by way of famine, war, pestilence, and death hint at the four horsemen of the apocalypse. While he is one hundred percent fiction, these horsemen are not. He will not send them out; on the contrary, it will be Jesus who does. One day the Lord will return and bring about a new and lasting order.

War, Fear, Famine, and Death

Revelation 6:1-8

> [1] *I watched as the Lamb opened the first of the seven seals. Then I heard one of the four living creatures say in a voice like thunder, "Come!"* [2] *I looked, and there before me was a white horse! Its rider held a bow, and he was given a crown, and he rode out as a conqueror bent on conquest.* [3] *When the Lamb opened the second seal, I heard the second living creature say, "Come!"* [4] *Then another horse came out, a fiery red one. Its rider was given power to take peace from the earth and to make men slay each other. To him was given a large sword.* [5] *When the Lamb opened the third seal, I heard the third living creature say, "Come!" I looked, and there before me was a black horse! Its rider was holding a pair of scales in his hand.* [6] *Then I heard what sounded like a voice among the four living creatures, saying, "A quart of wheat for a day's wages, and three quarts of barley for a day's wages, and do not damage the oil and the wine!"* [7] *When the Lamb opened the fourth seal, I heard the voice of the fourth living creature say, "Come!"* [8] *I looked, and there before me was a pale horse! Its rider was named Death, and Hades was following close behind him. They were given power over a fourth of the earth to kill by sword, famine and plague, and by the wild beasts of the earth.*

* **Revelation 6:1** → When the Lamb (Jesus) opens the first seal, the words on the scroll become a full-feature, cinematic experience for John. The apocalypse – meaning the disclosure of knowledge regarding end-time events on the earth and the second coming of Jesus to the earth – is what follows. This period of time in which God's judgment is poured out on the world, along with the rise of the Satan-empowered man referred to as the Antichrist, is referred to in the Bible as the Tribulation. For John to say that the living creature had a voice like thunder reveals his immense power. Most of us have experienced the deafening claps of thunder associated with lightning storms. Being outside when the cracks and booms sound off gives one a healthy appreciation of God's power. It also makes people seek safe shelter quickly! In the make-believe world of comics, there are characters such as Thor (called the god of thunder), Ororo (also known as Storm) and others who can control the elements. In the real heavenly dimension, John has seen and now hears one of the four living creatures, who's voice sounds like the crack and rumble of thunder. If the created beings have this much power, how much more infinitely greater is the One who sits on the throne (God the Father) and the Lamb (God the Son – Jesus the Savior)? Wow!

* **Revelation 6:2** → Next, John sees and relays to the readers of Revelation 6:2 four horses and four horsemen, each possessing defining characteristics and horrible judgments which they will pour out on the earth's inhabitants. Revelation 6:2-8 parallel what Jesus told his disciples in Matthew 24:4-31:

> Jesus answered: "Watch out that no one deceives you. For many will come in my name, claiming, 'I am the Messiah,' and will deceive many. You will hear of wars and rumors of wars, but see to it that you are not alarmed. Such things must happen, but the end is still to come. Nation will rise against nation, and kingdom against kingdom. There will be famines and earthquakes in various places. All these are the beginning of birth pains.

Then you will be handed over to be persecuted and put to death, and you will be hated by all nations because of me. At that time many will turn away from the faith and will betray and hate each other, and many false prophets will appear and deceive many people. Because of the increase of wickedness, the love of most will grow cold, but the one who stands firm to the end will be saved. And this gospel of the kingdom will be preached in the whole world as a testimony to all nations, and then the end will come.

So when you see standing in the holy place 'the abomination that causes desolation,' spoken of through the prophet Daniel—let the reader understand—then let those who are in Judea flee to the mountains. Let no one on the housetop go down to take anything out of the house. Let no one in the field go back to get their cloak. How dreadful it will be in those days for pregnant women and nursing mothers! Pray that your flight will not take place in winter or on the Sabbath. For then there will be great distress, unequaled from the beginning of the world until now—and never to be equaled again.

If those days had not been cut short, no one would survive, but for the sake of the elect those days will be shortened. At that time if anyone says to you, 'Look, here is the Messiah!' or, 'There he is!' do not believe it. For false messiahs and false prophets will appear and perform great signs and wonders to deceive, if possible, even the elect. See, I have told you ahead of time.

So if anyone tells you, 'There he is, out in the wilderness,' do not go out; or, 'Here he is, in the inner rooms,' do not believe it. For as lightning that comes from the east is visible even in the west, so will be the coming of the Son of Man. Wherever there is a carcass, there the vultures will gather.

Immediately after the distress of those days

'the sun will be darkened,
                and the moon will not give its light;

the stars will fall from the sky,
                and the heavenly bodies will be shaken.'

Then will appear the sign of the Son of Man in heaven. And then all the peoples of the earth will mourn when they see the Son of Man coming on the clouds of heaven, with power and great glory. And he will send his angels with a loud trumpet call, and they will gather his elect from the four winds, from one end of the heavens to the other."

The Antichrist

The first horse is white and ridden by a rider having a bow and crown. This horse and rider are not to be confused with the Rider and the white horse that are described in Revelation 19. That rider is the Lord Jesus Christ himself. The rider on the white horse in Revelation 6 is thought to be by many leading theologians as the Antichrist. They hold to this belief because he will come to power on earth during this time period called the Tribulation, when there will begin unprecedented global distress and strivings of nations (against one another) for economic, political, and technological superiority and survival. The Antichrist will emerge as the world leader and later deceive the nations, causing them to worship him and Satan. We will learn more about the Antichrist when we dive into Revelation 11:7, 13:3, and 17:8-9 - Scriptures that reveal more about this man referred to in the Bible as the man of lawlessness. As Jesus said in Matthew 24:4-5:

> Watch out that no one deceives you. For many will come in my name, claiming, "I am the Christ," and will deceive many.

The Tribulation is a seven-year period of time referred to in the Bible that will commence soon after the church is raptured out of the world. Soon afterwards, the man referred to as the Antichrist will be revealed. Whether the rider on the white horse is the Antichrist or representative of world leaders and/or heads of global military powers, the bow that he carries is a sign indicating that he is a warrior (for ignoble and satanic purposes). About the Antichrist, the Bible says:

> Concerning the coming of our Lord Jesus Christ and our being gathered to him, we ask you, brothers and sisters, not to become easily unsettled or alarmed by the teaching allegedly from us—whether by a prophecy or by word of mouth or by letter—asserting that the day of the Lord has already come. Don't let anyone deceive you in any way, for that day will not come until the rebellion occurs and the man of lawlessness is revealed, the man doomed to destruction. He will oppose and will exalt himself over everything that is called God or is worshiped, so that he sets himself up in God's temple, proclaiming himself to be God. Don't you remember that when I was with you I used to tell you these things? And

now you know what is holding him back, so that he may be revealed at the proper time. For the secret power of lawlessness is already at work; but the one who now holds it back will continue to do so till he is taken out of the way. And then the lawless one will be revealed, whom the Lord Jesus will overthrow with the breath of his mouth and destroy by the splendor of his coming. The coming of the lawless one will be in accordance with how Satan works. He will use all sorts of displays of power through signs and wonders that serve the lie, and all the ways that wickedness deceives those who are perishing. They perish because they refused to love the truth and so be saved. For this reason God sends them a powerful delusion so that they will believe the lie and so that all will be condemned who have not believed the truth but have delighted in wickedness. [II Thessalonians 2:1-12]

MUTANT INSIGHT

Professor X: "You're just another false god. And whoever is left to follow you when this is all over will betray you again."
Apocalypse: "You're wrong Charles. For the first time in a thousand lifetimes I have *you*. For all my gifts, I've yet to possess the one I needed most...to be everywhere, to be everyone!"

[X-Men: Apocalypse]

As Professor X wisely states, false gods are not worthy to be followed or worshiped. What is a false god? Anything or anyone that is exalted as the object of our worship, affections, desires, and sacrifice. Professor X understood the first and second of the Ten Commandments:

> You shall have no other gods before me. [Exodus 20:3]

> You shall not make for yourself an image in the form of anything in heaven above or on the earth beneath or in the waters below. You shall not bow down to them or worship them; for I, the Lord your God, am a jealous God, punishing the children for the sin of the parents to the third and fourth generation of those who hate me, but showing love to a thousand generations of those who love me and keep my commandments. [Exodus 20:4-6]

The wise person obeys the Lord and exalts no one as their supreme leader except him—regardless of the consequences. It is better to be rejected by others for not bowing to idols versus being rejected by God because we compromised by worshiping other gods.

The Coming Global Conflict

* **Revelation 6:3-4** → The rider on the fiery red horse represents the unprecedented wars, factions and conflicts that will occur during the seven-year period referred to in the Bible as the Tribulation years. Bloodshed will be rampant during this period of unrest on the earth, as represented by the fiery red color of this horse and the rider with the sword. Jesus foretold this in Matthew 24:6-7(a),

You will hear of wars and rumors of wars, but see to it that you are not alarmed. Such things must happen, but the end is still to come. Nation will rise against nation, and kingdom against kingdom.

* **Revelation 6:5-6** → The rider on the black horse represents the increased levels of famine that will be widespread across the world during the Tribulation period. Remember the first two horses and riders? When war comes, food often becomes in short supply. The scales being held by the rider tell us two things. One, there will be unjust dealings with the poor. Two, the cost of food will not be in balance with its true value; rather, greed and leverage (of the rule of the Antichrist) will oppress them. These verses reveal that most people's daily wages will only be just enough to eat for the day. This parallels what Jesus foretold in Matthew 24:7(b) [also see Matthew 24:11-22],

There will be famines and earthquakes in various places. All these are the beginning of birth pains.

* **Revelation 6:7-8** → When the fourth seal is opened, John sees a pale horse with Death riding on it, followed by Hades (the holding place of all who die and don't' know Jesus as Savior). Why is Hades following Death? Because when the body dies, the eternal souls of those who will not submit to Christ in this life go to this place of sorrow and torment. Disease and pestilence will ravage the earth during the time of the Tribulation.

Pale, the color of the fourth horse, symbolizes the death-like appearance of corpses. Today, people laugh, joke, and proclaim their "love" for zombies and end-of-the-world movies and television shows. They have been deceived to love what they should not. The time period of the Tribulation years will cause fear and desperation to run rampant due to real zombie-like conditions across the globe. Revelation 6:8 tells us that one-fourth of the world's population will be killed during this judgment. Consider this fact: "In June 2013, the Population Division of the United Nations Department of Economic and Social Affairs estimated the world population at approximately 7.2 billion."[7] At the time of the rapture, just prior to the Tribulation, millions of people who have surrendered to Jesus Christ as their Lord and Savior will be taken out of the world by God. So, using the 7.2 billion number, let's assume for illustration purposes that ten percent of that number (720 million people) are true followers of Christ and will be raptured. That would leave 6.5 billion people still on the earth to go through the Tribulation years.

According to what we've read in previous verses about the destruction that will be brought about by the four horses and horsemen, one-fourth of the 6.5 billion people (equates to 1.6 billion people) will be killed with the sword, famine, plagues, and wild beasts of the earth. Thus in this scenario, the world's population – minus raptured Christians and those killed by the sword, famine, plagues and wild beasts – would be reduced from 7.2 billion to 4.9 billion (a 32.5 percent world-population drop). And this is just the beginning of the end. Friend, if you have not surrendered your life to the love and salvation that God offers you in the Lord Jesus Christ, why not do so today? Tomorrow is not promised.

Chapter 15

Slain Souls and Heavenly Signs

Revelation 6:9-17

Apocalypse: "Those who oppose me shall perish through my agents of destruction: famine, pestilence, war, and my greatest creation...death..."

[X-Men The Animated Series: Come the Apocalypse]

Once again, the words of the fictional character Apocalypse spring from the pages of the Bible. Having just read the truth of God's Word as related to the four horses and horsemen, please know that one express purpose for my writing this book was to make clear to comic fans that the words above – found in comic books, cartoons, and the blockbuster movie *X-Men: Apocalypse* – are not fantasy. Unless Jesus is either a liar or a lunatic, these things will one day happen. And be not mistaken: He is neither liar nor lunatic. He is the Lord!

It is my hope that many who may be indifferent about Jesus and the Bible, yet actively read comics and wait with great excitement for the release of new comic-based action movies, will wake up from their spiritual slumber and actively grow in their love and knowledge of the Lord Jesus Christ.

The Great and Dreadful Day of the Lord

Revelation 6:9-17

[9] *When he opened the fifth seal, I saw under the altar the souls of those who had been slain because of the word of God and the testimony they had maintained.* [10] *They called out in a loud voice, "How long, Sovereign Lord, holy and true, until you judge the inhabitants of the earth and avenge our blood?"* [11] *Then each of them was given a white robe, and they were told to wait a little longer, until the number of their fellow servants and brothers who were to be killed as they had been was completed.* [12] *I watched as he opened the sixth seal. There was a great earthquake. The sun turned black like sackcloth made of goat hair, the whole moon turned blood red,* [13] *and the stars in the sky fell to earth, as late figs drop from a fig tree when shaken by a strong wind.* [14] *The sky receded like a scroll, rolling up, and every mountain and island was removed from its place.* [15] *Then the kings of the earth, the princes, the generals, the rich, the mighty, and every slave and every free man hid in caves and among the rocks of the mountains.* [16] *They called to the mountains and the rocks, "Fall on us and hide us from the face of him who sits on the throne and from the wrath of the Lamb!* [17] *For the great day of their wrath has come, and who can stand?*

* **Revelation 6:9-11** → While the first four seals judgments of God have to do with activities on the earth regarding sinful humans, the fifth seal judgment is about God's activity in heaven

regarding the souls of humans who had been murdered because of their faith in Jesus when they lived on the earth. Many Christians have been killed over the years for one reason – allegiance to Jesus. This is still happening in gruesome ways all over the world, but such killings will escalate exponentially during the Tribulation years. The faithfulness of these martyrs will result in eternal blessings and rewards that God will bestow upon them.

   * **Revelation 6:12-17** → The opening of the sixth seal ushers in a future period when God's judgment will be poured out on the earth. Jesus spoke about this period about two thousand years ago during his earthly ministry as the Lamb of God:

> There will be signs in the sun, moon and stars. On the earth, nations will be in anguish and perplexity at the roaring and tossing of the sea. People will faint from terror, apprehensive of what is coming on the world, for the heavenly bodies will be shaken. At that time they will see the Son of Man coming in a cloud with power and great glory. When these things begin to take place, stand up and lift up your heads, because your redemption is drawing near. [Luke 21:25-28]

The second coming of the Lord Jesus Christ to earth will be a mighty and glorious day for those who know Him as their Lord and Savior. At the culmination of the Tribulation years, just prior to Jesus' return, the earth and galaxy will be radically affected. But for those who do not know Him, however, his second coming will be a dreadful day. Verses 15-17 indicate when brazen and godless world leaders see Jesus when he comes again [Revelation 1:7-8; Zechariah 14:1-9], they will be terrified and gripped with fear.

Chapter 16

Signed, Sealed, Delivered – I'm Yours

Revelation 7:1-8

Charles Xavier: "Just because someone stumbles and loses their path doesn't mean they can't be saved."

[X-Men First Class]

Professor Xavier's words above are consistent with the truth of God's redemptive plan for mankind. John 3:16 says, "For God so loved the world that he gave his one and only Son, that whoever believes in him shall not perish but have eternal life." No matter how a person has blown it in this life, they can be saved by God's grace. Saved from what, you ask? Saved from the power of sin in this life and the penalty of sin for eternity in hell. How does one receive this salvation? The answer can be found in Romans 10:9-13:

> If you declare with your mouth, "Jesus is Lord," and believe in your heart that God raised him from the dead, you will be saved. For it is with your heart that you believe and are justified, and it is with your mouth that you profess your faith and are saved. As Scripture says, 'Anyone who believes in him will never be put to shame.' For there is no difference between Jew and Gentile—the same Lord is Lord of

all and richly blesses all who call on him, for, "Everyone who calls on the name of the Lord will be saved."

Four Angels and the Earth's Four Corners

Revelation 7:1-8

> [1] *After this I saw four angels standing at the four corners of the earth, holding back the four winds of the earth to prevent any wind from blowing on the land or on the sea or on any tree.* [2] *Then I saw another angel coming up from the east, having the seal of the living God. He called out in a loud voice to the four angels who had been given power to harm the land and the sea:* [3] *"Do not harm the land or the sea or the trees until we put a seal on the foreheads of the servants of our God."* [4] *Then I heard the number of those who were sealed: 144,000 from all the tribes of Israel.* [5] *From the tribe of Judah 12,000 were sealed, from the tribe of Reuben 12,000, from the tribe of Gad 12,000,* [6] *from the tribe of Asher 12,000, from the tribe of Naphtali 12,000, from the tribe of Manasseh 12,000,* [7] *from the tribe of Simeon 12,000, from the tribe of Levi 12,000, from the tribe of Issachar 12,000,* [8] *from the tribe of Zebulun 12,000, from the tribe of Joseph 12,000, from the tribe of Benjamin 12,000.*

  * Revelation 7:1 → John sees four angels (not the four living creatures) standing at the earth's four corners. Some might be saying right about now, "See, look at this made-up, antiquated nonsense! Everyone knows the earth is not flat; so what's this nonsense about four corners? You can't believe the Bible!" So the question is this: Is the statement in this verse regarding the "four corners of the earth" true? Let's dive into this and find out if the reliability of the Bible can indeed be trusted. The fact is that the Bible never references the earth as being flat. On the contrary, this what the Bible says about the circular shape of the earth:

> Do you not know? Have you not heard? Has it not been told you from the beginning? Have you not understood since the earth was founded? He sits enthroned above *the circle of the earth*, and its people are like grasshoppers. He stretches out the heavens like a canopy, and spreads them out like a tent to live in. [Isaiah 40:21-22, emphasis added]

So, if the earth is round, what's up with the four corners of the earth statement? In answering this logical question, we will see that faith and science are validated as *not* being opposed to each other. God has not asked us to "check our brains" at the door and live with a blind, ignorant, and non-questioning faith.

By way of measurements made by earth-circling satellites, scientists have actually proven that the earth indeed has four corners (referred to also as pyramid-shaped high points). In an article entitled, "Earth Has Four Corners", published in the Science News Letter, June 19, 1965:

> The Earth has four corners, measurements made of earth-circling satellites have shown. The high points each cover several thousand square miles of the earth's surface. They are 220 feet higher than they would be if the earth were exactly spherical. The low areas between the high points are about

253 feet below what would be expected if the world were precisely round. The four-cornered, or pyramid-like, design was found by calculating the changes in the orbits of globe-girdling satellites. At the center of the high points, the satellites were pulled downward a few hundred feet by the unexpectedly high gravity. The new findings give the earth four known superimposed shapes: (1) It bulges at the equator, as has been known for a long time. (2) It is slightly pear-shaped, with the narrow end in the Arctic and the broad base in the Antarctic. (3) The earth's equator is egg-shaped, not circular. (4) It has four high points, roughly of pyramid shape.

One of the earth's high points centers over Ireland in the Northern Hemisphere and sprawls northward toward the pole. Another extends across the equator from New Guinea northward toward Japan. A third corner is south of Africa centered about halfway to Antarctica, and the fourth corner of the pyramid is west of South America, with the high point off Peru. The new figure for the earth was found by scientists at Johns Hopkins Applied Physics Laboratory in Silver Spring, Md., working under contract for the U.S. Navy's Bureau of Naval Weapons. Dr. Robert R. Newton, with Drs. William H Guier and George C. Weiffenbach, directed the studies. Ever since Magellan proved that the earth is round, scientists have been trying to prove that he was wrong. Although they have been successful, the imperfections from a sphere are minor considering the earth's vast size, nearly 25,000 miles around the equator, with an area of nearly 197 million square miles."[8] [9]

So, the words of Revelation 7:1 are consistent with scientific facts and global realities. Once again it is proven that the Bible and science are not in conflict at all. Having addressed the "four corners of the earth" reference in the first part of the verse, consider next the deep implications of what God has commanded these four angels to do: prevent the winds of the earth to blow on land, sea, or trees.

MUTANT INSIGHT

Apocalypse: You had your chance to be the first of my creatures, the first to serve my will!
Rogue: Dang, I missed it!

[X-Men The Animated Series: Come the Apocalypse]

In the episode prior to one that includes the dialogue above, Rogue almost succumbed to the deception of Apocalypse. This would have led her into the dark world of being one of his horsemen of evil. She was susceptible to his deceptive tactics due to her feelings of inadequacy and not being "normal". With her particular mutant power, she could never physically touch anyone else because their thoughts, emotions, memories, and powers (if they had any) would be transferred to her. The weight of carrying other people's life issues was tough enough. But much worse were her fears of never being able to draw close to someone and experience real love.

Rogue believed that with her powers, she would always be alone and not know love. Thanks to Professor X, she learned that this belief was not completely true. She decided to embrace who she was and open her eyes to all of the loving relationships in her life. She resisted the downward pull of the darkness, which promises a lot but delivers very little that truly satisfies our souls. Do as Rogue did: resist Satan's deceptive attacks on your mind and life. As she trusted Professor X to guide and help her, trust God to make you into a new creation:

> Therefore, if anyone is in Christ, the new creation has come: The old has gone, the new is here!"
> [II Corinthians 5:17]

Atmospheric Disruptions

Let's circle back around to the four angels of Revelation 7:1 and what God has commanded them to do: prevent wind from blowing on the earth. First, what is wind? All people experience it, but may not understand what it is. A simple explanation is this: as the sun heats the earth, it creates convection currents which, due to the earth's rotation, begin to spin. As the spinning currents begin to randomly spread, they cause the effects we experience as wind. When the wind ceases to blow, one effect is that rainfall over dry land will become rare – due to the fact that the wind would not be blowing clouds from over oceans (where they form) to land.

The lack of rainfall will negatively affect vegetation growth, crippling the food supply. In addition, the growth and life of trees, plants, and grass will be adversely affected. This in turn will cause oxygen production to be reduced, leaving an over-abundance of carbon dioxide breathed out by humans and animals, negatively impacting the atmosphere. Another area of great concern will be the rise of extreme temperatures. With no wind, the areas under the sun will become much hotter and the areas where there is no sun will become much colder. In summary, the lack of wind will be devastating on the world's population. God is trumpeting warnings via the book of the Revelation. Turn to Jesus!

   * **Revelation 7:2-8** → As we've discussed, the rapture is the defining event that will mark the end of the church era and usher in seven years referred to as the Tribulation period. This is a future period when God's judgment will be poured out on earth due to mankind's disobedience and rebellion. During the seven years of the Tribulation, God will be especially focused on the nation of Israel. He will select 12,000 from each of the twelve tribes of Israel to be his specially selected ambassadors to proclaim of the message of repentance and salvation in the Lord Jesus Christ. The scene in Revelation 7:2-8 is like a pause in God's judgment that will be poured out on the rebellious and wicked world. The four angels standing at the four corners of the earth have been given power to hold back the winds from blowing on the land, sea or trees and thus harm the earth. However, before they are allowed to do so, these 144,000 servants of God must receive the seal of God (signifying ownership and allegiance) so that they will be protected and unharmed from any of the judgments falling on the world.

Chapter 17

The Heavenly White Linen Party

Revelation 7:9-17

Apocalypse: "Beware of what you ask for, for it may come to pass."

[X-Men The Animated Series: Obsession]

Apocalypse's words are directed to Wolverine, who wanted to participate in the action of fighting him. While Wolverine is a formidable fighter and virtually incapable of dying or remaining injured, to think that he can do more than merely scratch Apocalypse is foolish thinking. Many people may be able to personally relate to the statement above, perhaps having "bitten off more than they could chew" in some endeavor they realized they weren't quite prepared. Many failures come about in life because emotions and feelings lead people to make ill-fated decisions.

Now consider your spiritual life. Rejecting God's love and offer to pardon you from the penalty of your sin is not wise. At the second coming of the Lord Jesus, the world will shout against him in a similar way as the mob did who called for his death [see Luke 23:20-25], shouting, "Crucify, crucify!" The Bible says at Jesus' second coming, the leaders and armies of the world will ban together to fight against him—to their own peril and eternal destruction. He will come as the unstoppable conqueror, not a Lamb to be slain again. Submit to his lordship and love today.

The Great Multitude in White Robes

Revelation 7:9-17

⁹After this I looked and there before me was a great multitude that no one could count, from every nation, tribe, people and language, standing before the throne and in front of the Lamb. They were wearing white robes and were holding palm branches in their hands. ¹⁰And they cried out in a loud voice: "Salvation belongs to our God, who sits on the throne, and to the Lamb." ¹¹All the angels were standing around the throne and around the elders and the four living creatures. They fell down on their faces before the throne and worshiped God, ¹²saying: "Amen! Praise and glory and wisdom and thanks and honor and power and strength be to our God for ever and ever. Amen!" ¹³Then one of the elders asked me, "These in white robes—who are they, and where did they come from?" ¹⁴I answered, "Sir, you know." And he said, "These are they who have come out of the great tribulation; they have washed their robes and made them white in the blood of the Lamb. ¹⁵Therefore, "they are before the throne of God and serve him day and night in his temple; and he who sits on the throne will spread his tent over them. ¹⁶Never again will they hunger; never again will they thirst. The sun will not beat upon them, nor any scorching heat. ¹⁷For the Lamb at the center of the throne will be their shepherd; he will lead

> *them to springs of living water. And God will wipe*
> *away every tear from their eyes."*

* **Revelation 7:9-17** → In verse nine, John sees a vast, diverse, and seemingly innumerable group of people before the throne of God. In speaking with one of the twenty-four elders who sit around the throne of God, John is told who this vast group is. They are people who have been killed because of their faith in Jesus Christ during the Great Tribulation years. Remember, the period referred to as "the Tribulation" is the first 3.5 years that follow the rapture of the church. The Great Tribulation is the 3.5 year period that follows the Tribulation period. The Antichrist will kill all who do not bow down to him (we will read more about this later). However, God is faithful and his redemptive plan is right on schedule.

Chapter 18

Silence of the Lamb's Followers

Revelation 8:1-13

Apocalypse: "All who oppose me shall be crushed!"

[X-Men The Animated Series: Come the Apocalypse]

Apocalypse's desire to conquer and rule has nothing to do with honor, righteousness, or love for others. He captures, enslaves, and kills others for his demented and selfish purposes. Not so the case with God, who has expressed His love to the world by clothing himself in flesh and living as a man for one purpose: to offer Himself as the perfect sacrifice to redeem mankind from the clutches of sin and death. The Bible states, "For there is one God and one mediator between God and mankind, the man Christ Jesus, who gave himself as a ransom for all people. This has now been witnessed to at the proper time." [I Timothy 2:5-6]

God has no desire to crush people. His desire is to rescue them from the deception, power, and penalty of sin. All who reject His offer of forgiveness and reconciliation, however, will indeed be dashed to pieces. Hebrews 10:31 warns all who stubbornly walk in defiance to God and thumb their nose at the sacrifice that Jesus made for them: "It is a dreadful thing to fall into the hands of the living God."

The Seventh Seal and the Golden Censer

Revelation 8:1-5

> [1] *When he opened the seventh seal, there was si-
> lence in heaven for about half an hour.* [2] *And I saw
> the seven angels who stand before God, and to
> them were given seven trumpets.* [3] *Another angel,
> who had a golden censer, came and stood at the
> altar. He was given much incense to offer, with
> the prayers of all the saints, on the golden altar
> before the throne.* [4] *The smoke of the incense, to-
> gether with the prayers of the saints, went up be-
> fore God from the angel's hand.* [5] *Then the angel
> took the censer, filled it with fire from the altar,
> and hurled it on the earth; and there came peals
> of thunder, rumblings, flashes of lightning and
> an earthquake.*

* Revelation 8:1-5 → Thus far in the reading of the Apocalypse (Revelation) of the Lord Jesus Christ, there have been many references to majestic sounds in heaven. These sounds have included God's voice, multitudes of people singing and praising God, mighty angels with booming voices, powerful living beasts with loud flapping wings, and loud cracks of thunder. In Revelation 8:1, however, the Lamb of God opens the seventh seal and, instead of majestic sounds as heard before, all of heaven goes silent for about thirty minutes. Whoa! This means that there is some serious stuff about to go down. The wise person will pay attention; the foolish will not.

Revelation 8 begins at the end of the Tribulation (3.5 years after it began) and now the period referred to as the Great Tribulation period (that will last another 3.5 years) begins. The fire-filled censer that the angel hurls on the earth begins a time of great natural disasters and adverse effects on nature. God has spoken and these things *will* come to pass just as he has sovereignly decreed. You must know Jesus Christ if you are to escape the coming judgment on this world.

The Trumpets

Revelation 8:6-11

> [6] *Then the seven angels who had the seven trumpets prepared to sound them.* [7] *The first angel sounded his trumpet, and there came hail and fire mixed with blood, and it was hurled down upon the earth. A third of the earth was burned up, a third of the trees were burned up, and all the green grass was burned up.* [8] *The second angel sounded his trumpet, and something like a huge mountain, all ablaze, was thrown into the sea. A third of the sea turned into blood,* [9] *a third of the living creatures in the sea died, and a third of the ships were destroyed.* [10] *The third angel sounded his trumpet, and a great star, blazing like a torch, fell from the sky on a third of the rivers and on the springs of water—* [11] *the name of the star is Wormwood. A third of the waters turned bitter, and many people died from the waters that had become bitter.*

* **Revelation 8:6-7** → These verses inform us that during the Great Tribulation (the second 3.5 years of the seven-year Tribulation period), a third of the earth will be burned up, a third of the trees will be burned up, and all the green grass will be burned up. This judgment is similar to God's judgment on Egypt during Moses' time, when God delivered the Israelites out of slavery and cruel bondage:

> Then the Lord said to Moses, "Stretch out your hand toward the sky so that hail will fall all over Egypt— on people and animals and on everything growing in the fields of Egypt." When Moses stretched out his staff toward the sky, the Lord sent thunder and hail, and lightning flashed down to the ground. So the Lord rained hail on the land of Egypt; hail fell and lightning flashed back and forth. It was the worst storm in all the land of Egypt since it had become a nation. Throughout Egypt hail struck everything in the fields—both people and animals; it beat down everything growing in the fields and stripped every tree. The only place it did not hail was the land of Goshen, where the Israelites were. [Exodus 9:22-26]

Think about the devastating ramifications of this first trumpet judgment, as related to atmospheric disruptions. Not only will there be smoke filling the skies, but also the process of photosynthesis (production of oxygen by plants and trees) will be severely impacted, just as described in Revelation 7 when the four angels prevented the wind from blowing. The ease of breathing clean air will, therefore, become a challenge for everyone. Additionally, with no grass, many animals will not survive. This, in turn, will impact food supplies for humans. The entire ecosystem will be thrown off, affecting birds, bugs, and other life on earth.

* **Revelation 8:8-9** → The second trumpet judgment targets the sea. Bible scholars agree that the linguistic context of the word "sea" in these verses refer to one sea – the Mediterranean Sea. Could the fiercely-burning, mountain-like object be an

asteroid hurled to the earth by the second angel? Remember, angels have immense powers like what we see in fictional comic book characters. We don't know. But the result is that one-third of sea life will be killed. The destruction of one-third of the ships means that many, many people will die too, as a result of being on and near the ships at the time of their destruction.

Countries having a coastline on the Mediterranean Sea include Spain, France, Monaco, Italy, Slovenia, Croatia, Bosnia and Herzegovina, Montenegro, Albania, Greece, Turkey, Syria, Lebanon, Israel, Palestine, Morocco, Algeria, Tunisia, Libya, Egypt, Malta, Cyprus, and Northern Cyprus. Commodities necessary for life and business will be destroyed and the effect on millions will be both immediate and devastating. It will truly be a time of great tribulation.

* **Revelation 8:10-11** → With the third trumpet judgment, the world's drinking water will be affected. This great star blazing like a torch could be a meteoroid that falls from the heavenly realm, breaking into smaller meteorites. On the other hand, it could be another God-created object, or even angel, used by God specifically for this period of judgment. In our world today, wormwood is a bitter and harmful plant used in the manufacture of absinthe, an intoxicating and very toxic beverage.

The Talking Eagle

Revelation 8:12-13

[12] *The fourth angel sounded his trumpet, and a third of the sun was struck, a third of the moon, and a third of the stars, so that a third of them turned dark. A third of the day was without light, and also a third of the night.* [13] *As I watched, I heard an eagle that was flying in midair call out*

in a loud voice: "Woe! Woe! Woe to the inhabitants of the earth, because of the trumpet blasts about to be sounded by the other three angels!"

* **Revelation 8:12** → The fourth trumpet judgment brings reduced light (and heat) to the world – during both the daytime and nighttime. The ramifications are deep here too. A third of the daytime light (four hours) and a third of the nighttime light (four hours) will be "turned off". The negative impact on the environment, people's mental state, along with rebellion, looting, and overall chaos will be some of the issues that will arise on the earth due to this fourth trumpet judgment.

* **Revelation 8:13** → It's going to be bad enough on earth after the first four trumpet judgments, but Revelation 8:13 indicates things will escalate and grow even worse. Remember that God will not pour out His judgment on the earth this way because he is a mean and unloving. No, He has both said and proven that he loves his creation. But just as earthly authorities set up rules and laws, expecting people to abide by them or suffer the consequences, there are severe consequences for those who rebel against God and choose to walk in disobedience.

Again, this sense of justice and eradicating evil is not something mankind generally objects too – except when it comes to God and his rules. What do I mean? Well, any of us shopping at stores or visiting museums aren't offended by the presence of video cameras and security guards. We also flock to see movies in which heroes work hard to uphold the law and bring wicked people to justice. Jesus, as the Hero of all heroes, will do nothing less than this – judge sin and deal sternly with all who reject his lordship.

Chapter 19

Smoke of Horrors

Revelation 9:1-21

Apocalypse: "I know more of this world than you can even dream... that is why I must destroy it."

[X-Men The Animated Series: The Cure]

In the comic world, Apocalypse knows more than other mutants and humans—but not because he is eternal or omniscient (all knowing). He knows more than other mutants and humans because he has been able to live through multiple centuries and gathered knowledge over this time. He remains confined to time and is neither omniscient nor omnipresent. In contrast, God almighty has no restrictions or limitations.

When speaking of destroying the world, Apocalypse doesn't actually want to eradicate all life. Having been taught to be strong to survive the extreme desert conditions of ancient Egypt where he was born and raised, his outlook on life has been shaped by the idea that "only the strong survive" (humans and mutants). He continually tests how fit individuals are. If someone survives multiple attacks, they are deemed more fit and worthy to live.

God knows all about the sin and depravity in the world, but he will not utterly destroy it. Rather, because of his great love, mercy, and grace, he will redeem mankind and creation from its fallen state brought on by sin. Read II Peter 3:1-14!

Scorpion-Like Creatures from the Abyss

Revelation 9:1-12

¹ *The fifth angel sounded his trumpet, and I saw a star that had fallen from the sky to the earth. The star was given the key to the shaft of the Abyss.* ² *When he opened the Abyss, smoke rose from it like the smoke from a gigantic furnace. The sun and sky were darkened by the smoke from the Abyss.* ³ *And out of the smoke locusts came down upon the earth and were given power like that of scorpions of the earth.* ⁴ *They were told not to harm the grass of the earth or any plant or tree, but only those people who did not have the seal of God on their foreheads.* ⁵ *They were not given power to kill them, but only to torture them for five months. And the agony they suffered was like that of the sting of a scorpion when it strikes a man.* ⁶ *During those days men will seek death, but will not find it; they will long to die, but death will elude them.* ⁷ *The locusts looked like horses prepared for battle. On their heads they wore something like crowns of gold, and their faces resembled human faces.* ⁸ *Their hair was like women's hair, and their teeth were like lions' teeth.* ⁹ *They had breastplates like breastplates of iron, and the sound of their wings was like the thundering of many horses and chariots rushing into battle.* ¹⁰ *They had tails and stings like scorpions,*

and in their tails they had power to torment peo-
*ple for five months. * [11] *They had as king over them*
the angel of the Abyss, whose name in Hebrew is
*Abaddon, and in Greek, Apollyon. * [12] *The first woe*
is past; two other woes are yet to come.

* **Revelation 9:1** → Remember the closing words of Revelation 8 were, "..."Woe! Woe! Woe to the inhabitants of the earth, because of the trumpet blasts about to be sounded by the other three angels!" Well, here is what will happen when the fifth Trumpet Judgment of God takes place on earth. The "star" mentioned in Revelation 9:1 is a divine agent sent to earth by God, presumably an angel. Keep in mind that John was using the language and understanding of people during his time (approximately A.D. 96). Imagine if someone with a smart-phone could go back in time to when John was alive and asked him to describe what he saw (a cell phone being used). His explanation would only give a shadow of what the device is, due to him never having seen one before and being overwhelmed with the realities of what he saw and heard. The same logic applies here. The heavenly being John sees flying down from the sky to earth was no doubt glowing with great radiance and power, which is why John describes him as a star.

* **Revelation 9:2** → The Abyss is not the same place as the what the Bible refers to as the final place of condemnation—hell (Greek word Gehenna). Scripture describes hell as the eternal lake of fire where Satan, all evil angels, and all who reject Christ as Savior will one day be. Gehenna is empty right now; no one is there. One day, however, it will hold many forever and ever. The Abyss, referred to in this chapter, is different. It is a holding place for rebellious angels, other evil agents and, one day, Satan [see Revelation 20] for a "brief period" (one thousand years). After this thousand-years period, Satan will be set free for a short while and then be cast into the eternal lake of fire forever. This will be discussed later in the review of Revelation 20. The original Greek word that is translated Abyss is *abussos*, meaning bottomless. It is a place that demons dread, as outlined in Luke 8:26-33:

> They sailed to the region of the Gerasenes, which is across the lake from Galilee. When Jesus stepped ashore, he was met by a demon-possessed man from the town. For a long time this man had not worn clothes or lived in a house, but had lived in the tombs. When he saw Jesus, he cried out and fell at his feet, shouting at the top of his voice, "What do you want with me, Jesus, Son of the Most High God? I beg you, don't torture me!" For Jesus had commanded the impure spirit to come out of the man. Many times it had seized him, and though he was chained hand and foot and kept under guard, he had broken his chains and had been driven by the demon into solitary places. Jesus asked him, "What is your name?" "Legion," he replied, because many demons had gone into him. And they begged Jesus repeatedly not to order them to go into the Abyss. A large herd of pigs was feeding there on the hillside. The demons begged Jesus to let them go into the pigs, and he gave them permission. When the demons came out of the man, they went into the pigs, and the herd rushed down the steep bank into the lake and was drowned.

* Revelation 9:3-12 → Revelation 9:11 indicates that an angel named Abaddon, or Apollyon (meaning "Destroyer"), will be the leader of the locust-like creatures from the Abyss. God has revealed all of these things in His Word so that we will know ahead of time what will take place and can choose to either to submit to his Lordship or reject him. As we reviewed in

Revelation 1:3, God says, "Blessed is the one who reads aloud the words of this prophecy, and blessed are those who hear it and take to heart what is written in it, because the time is near."

The Four Angels Bound at the Euphrates River

Revelation 9:13-21

> [13] *The sixth angel sounded his trumpet, and I heard a voice coming from the horns of the golden altar that is before God.* [14] *It said to the sixth angel who had the trumpet, "Release the four angels who are bound at the great river Euphrates."* [15] *And the four angels who had been kept ready for this very hour and day and month and year were released to kill a third of mankind.* [16] *The number of the mounted troops was two hundred million. I heard their number.* [17] *The horses and riders I saw in my vision looked like this: Their breastplates were fiery red, dark blue, and yellow as sulfur. The heads of the horses resembled the heads of lions, and out of their mouths came fire, smoke and sulfur.* [18] *A third of mankind was killed by the three plagues of fire, smoke and sulfur that came out of their mouths.* [19] *The power of the horses was in their mouths and in their tails; for their tails were like snakes, having heads with which they inflict injury.* [20] *The rest of mankind that were not killed by these plagues still did not repent of the work of their hands; they did not stop worshiping demons, and idols of gold, silver, bronze, stone and wood—idols that cannot see or hear or walk.* [21] *Nor did they repent of their mur-*

*ders, their magic arts, their sexual immorality or
their thefts.*

* **Revelation 9:13-21** → After blowing his trumpet, the sixth
angel is told to release four evil angels who are bound at the
Euphrates River. As with everything else, the four angels will be
released according to God's eternal and sovereign timetable. The
two hundred-million-member army that these four evil angels
will lead ride on horses that are different in genetic make-up than
horses on earth; they have fire, smoke, and sulfur coming from
their mouths.

Just to get a sense of the impact these trumpet judgments
will have on the human population, let's circle back to what
was discussed when examining Revelation 6:7-8. Recall the 4.9
billion people (in our example) that would still be left on the
earth after the rapture and the fourth seal judgment. With this in
mind, Revelation 6:18 states yet another one-third of mankind
will be killed by the power of the horses' mouths. Considering
the hypothetical scenario pointed out in the review of Revelation
6:7-8 (the beginning of the earth's population decimation due to
global judgments from God) this equates to another 1.6 billion
people losing their lives. In our scenario, this would leave 3.2
billion people on the earth after this sixth Trumpet Judgment.
Thus, from the time of the Rapture of the Church through this
future point in time, 55 percent of the world's population will be
gone – a reduction from 7.2 billion to 3.2 billion people.

After all that is going to happens in Revelation 9:2-19, John
pens the amazingly sad words of 9:20-21, where the remaining
global population defiantly refuses to repent of their sins and
turn to God. Wow! Some readers may have been asking earlier,
'Why is God so judgmental?' Now you know why. The Lord
is, indeed, loving, kind, gracious, and merciful. He proved it by
sacrificially dying for us when he did not have to, while people
were in a rebellious and sinful state. Re-read 2 Peter 3 (found

in our discussion of Revelation 16). God is patient, not wanting any to perish. However, he is also just, He is righteous, He is holy...He is God! The ungodly, those who refuse to worship him and submit to his authority, will one day stand before him and be judged.

This is not a scenario beyond one's grasp of thinking or acceptance. Mankind has laws, authorities, judges, juries, and consequences that deal with rebels and lawbreakers – and people are generally glad for it. God is no different. He *will* one day (possibly sooner than the world thinks) return in ultimate splendor, majesty, and power to deal with rebels and lawbreakers. Surrender to him and share the good news with others so that they can come to know him as Savior, Friend, and Master.

Chapter 20

The Giant Angel and the Little Scroll

Revelation 10:1-11

MUTANT INSIGHT

Apocalypse: "Fool, you dare to claim dominion over me?"

[X-Men The Animated Series: Time Fugitives, Part 1]

The words of Apocalypse ring out to his opposition, exclaiming that anyone who tries to exact control, rule, or mastery over him is a fool. In essence, he is saying that anyone who has seen his power, yet dares to go against him is not wise. The sad reality is that during the period of Jesus' arrest, beatings, and crucifixion, wicked people dared to claim dominion over him. In the future, at His second coming, most of the world will foolishly again try to subdue Him and claim dominion over Him by fighting against Him. However, they will quickly learn that while he willfully allowed them to have dominion over Him at his crucifixion, He will be the unstoppable One at His return. He will have dominion over all of his adversaries for all of eternity. Read Psalm 2:1-12; here are verses 10-12:

> Therefore, you kings, be wise; be warned, you rulers of the earth. Serve the Lord with fear and celebrate his rule with trembling. Kiss his son, or he will be angry and your way will lead to your destruction,

for his wrath can flare up in a moment. Blessed are all who take refuge in him.

The Giant Angel and the Little Scroll

Revelation 10:1-5

> [1] *Then I saw another mighty angel coming down from heaven. He was robed in a cloud, with a rainbow above his head; his face was like the sun, and his legs were like fiery pillars.* [2] *He was holding a little scroll, which lay open in his hand. He planted his right foot on the sea and his left foot on the land,* [3] *and he gave a loud shout like the roar of a lion. When he shouted, the voices of the seven thunders spoke.* [4] *And when the seven thunders spoke, I was about to write; but I heard a voice from heaven say, "Seal up what the seven thunders have said and do not write it down."* [5] *Then the angel I had seen standing on the sea and on the land raised his right hand to heaven.*

* **Revelation 10:1** → Over the years, television shows and movies have utilized more and more the powerful visual effects of computer generated imaging (CGI). By way of this technology, entertainment producers are able to create phenomenal special effects – including powerful fictitious beings that include superheroes. In Revelation 10:1, however, John was seeing the real deal; a mighty angel from a different dimension (heaven) with power and splendor that no one can conceive. The description of his face and legs speaks of the heavenly glory and radiant splendor that he possesses. It could possibly mean that this angel has a look similar to the Human Torch. Consider these verses:

> He [God] makes winds his messengers, flames of fire his servants. [Psalm 104:4]

> In speaking of the angels he says, "He makes his angels spirits, and his servants flames of fire." [Hebrews 1:7]

   * **Revelation 10:2-5** → Note in Revelation 10:2 and 10:5 that the angel has one foot on the land and the other foot *on*, not *in*, the sea. He is standing *on* the water – a being not subject to the same gravitational laws to which we are bound. Because this being has one foot on the sea and the other on the land, the implication is that he is huge – such as the size of the fictional superhero called Giant Man. The sound of thunder is often connected to the voice of God's judgment:

> When he thunders, the waters in the heavens roar; he makes clouds rise from the ends of the earth. He sends lightning with the rain and brings out the wind from his storehouses. [Jeremiah 10:13]

> Listen closely to the thunder of His voice, and the rumbling that goes out from His mouth. Under the whole heaven He lets it loose, and His lightning to the ends of the earth. After it, a voice roars; He thunders with His majestic voice, and He does not restrain the lightnings when His voice is heard. God thunders with His voice wondrously, doing great things which we cannot comprehend. [Job 37:2-5]

The Sweet N' Sour Honey Scroll

Revelation 10:6-11

> [6] *And he swore by him who lives for ever and ever, who created the heavens and all that is in them, the earth and all that is in it, and the sea and all that is in it, and said, "There will be no more delay!* [7] *But in the days when the seventh angel is about to sound his trumpet, the mystery of God will be accomplished, just as he announced to his servants the prophets."* [8] *Then the voice that I had heard from heaven spoke to me once more: "Go, take the scroll that lies open in the hand of the angel who is standing on the sea and on the land."* [9] *So I went to the angel and asked him to give me the little scroll. He said to me, "Take it and eat it. It will turn your stomach sour, but in your mouth it will be as sweet as honey."* [10] *I took the little scroll from the angel's hand and ate it. It tasted as sweet as honey in my mouth, but when I had eaten it, my stomach turned sour.* [11] *Then I was told, "You must prophesy again about many peoples, nations, languages and kings."*

* Revelation 10:6-7 → The mighty angel's last six words in verse six are emphatic and clear. The question is this: are people listening? The "mystery of God" that is mentioned in verse seven refers to what is written in Colossians 1:24-28:

> Now I rejoice in what I am suffering for you, and I fill up in my flesh what is still lacking in regard to Christ's afflictions, for the sake of his body, which is the church. I have become its servant by the com-

mission God gave me to present to you the word of God in its fullness— the mystery that has been kept hidden for ages and generations, but is now disclosed to the Lord's people. To them God has chosen to make known among the Gentiles the glorious riches of this mystery, which is Christ in you, the hope of glory.

Reading the book of Revelation should cause us to humble ourselves before God and marvel at Him. One day, at his second coming, the Lord Jesus Christ will be seen for who he is: the glorious and all-powerful God of the Universe. Sonic booms, heavenly trumpets, flashes of lightning, and mighty angels will announce his grand entrance. Then Jesus, the majestic King of all kings, will appear.

All of this is evidence that God's judgment is right, and as a result you will be counted worthy of the kingdom of God, for which you are suffering. God is just: He will pay back trouble to those who trouble you and give relief to you who are troubled, and to us as well. This will happen when the Lord Jesus is revealed from heaven in blazing fire with his powerful angels. He will punish those who do not know God and do not obey the gospel (truth) of our Lord Jesus. They will be punished with everlasting destruction and shut out from the presence of the Lord and from the majesty of his power on the day he comes to be glorified in his holy people and to be marveled at among all those who have believed. [II Thessalonians 1:5-10]

* **Revelation 10:8-11** → John was being prepared to see, hear and write more about God's future judgment. He was available,

attentive, and obedient to God's words and instructions. If we are available and attentive, we, too, will also hear God calling us – for both general and specific to-do's as his ambassadors in this world [II Corinthians 5:20].

Chapter 21

The Super-Powered Duo

Revelation 11:1-19

Apocalypse: "Return to me, O sweet Death, my Horseman, and all shall be forgiven!"
Archangel: "Forgiven? You ruined my life!"
Apocalypse: "Ruined? No. I created a slave of you – yes, but a slave of courage and fire!

[X-Men The Animated Series: Obsession]

In the exchange above, Apocalypse states in his demented way that he is willing to forgive his horseman who rebelled against him. Real forgiveness, however, never manifests itself in ways that enslaves others. No, slavery is all about dominating and manipulating others for personal gain. Apocalypse is power-hungry, egotistical, selfish, and ruthless. He steals, kills, and destroys.

Moving beyond this evil fictional character's twisted understanding of forgiveness, the Bible makes clear that there are adversaries who desire to condemn people to lives of bondage and slavery. The outward adversaries are Satan and his emissaries. The inward adversary is each person's own sinful nature. One must be vigilant about not allowing the deceiving tactics of Satan or the wicked desires of their own heart to lead them into emotional, mental, and eternal dungeons.

Satan has deceived masses of people into believing that if they submit to God and his plan, then their lives will be ruined because they will have to be "do-gooders" and miss out on fun in life by getting on the "straight-and-narrow path" [see Matthew 7:13-14]. However, if Professor X, Cyclops, Beast, and all their superhero colleagues were real, they would say that hundreds of millions of people across the globe adore and cheer them as superheroes because they (the heroes) are do-gooders who live upright! In fact, the straight-and-narrow is quite cool. These superheroes have chosen to become "slaves" of goodness, not evil. This is a Biblical concept! Check out Romans 6:20-23:

> When you were slaves to sin, you were free from the control of righteousness. What benefit did you reap at that time from the things you are now ashamed of? Those things result in death! But now that you have been set free from sin and have become slaves of God, the benefit you reap leads to holiness, and the result is eternal life. For the wages of sin is death, but the gift of God is eternal life in Christ Jesus our Lord.

Superheroes would never go into battle against dangerous foes without properly preparing. Just as many of them have to suit up to do battle in the realm of fiction, we are commanded to do the same in real life. The Bible instructs all followers of Jesus Christ to:

> Finally, be strong in the Lord and in his mighty power. Put on the full armor of God, so that you can take your stand against the devil's schemes. For our struggle is not against flesh and blood, but against the rulers, against the authorities, against the powers of this dark world and against the spiritual

forces of evil in the heavenly realms. Therefore put on the full armor of God, so that when the day of evil comes, you may be able to stand your ground, and after you have done everything, to stand. Stand firm then, with the belt of truth buckled around your waist, with the breastplate of righteousness in place, and with your feet fitted with the readiness that comes from the gospel of peace. In addition to all this, take up the shield of faith, with which you can extinguish all the flaming arrows of the evil one. Take the helmet of salvation and the sword of the Spirit, which is the word of God. And pray in the Spirit on all occasions with all kinds of prayers and requests. With this in mind, be alert and always keep on praying for all the Lord's people. [Ephesians 6:10-18]

Super-Powered By God

Revelation 11:1-6

[1] *I was given a reed like a measuring rod and was told, "Go and measure the temple of God and the altar, and count the worshipers there. [2] But exclude the outer court; do not measure it, because it has been given to the Gentiles. They will trample on the holy city for 42 months. [3] And I will give power to my two witnesses, and they will prophesy for 1,260 days, clothed in sackcloth." [4] These are the two olive trees and the two lampstands that stand before the Lord of the earth. [5] If anyone tries to harm them, fire comes from their mouths*

and devours their enemies. This is how anyone who wants to harm them must die. ⁶ These men have power to shut up the sky so that it will not rain during the time they are prophesying; and they have power to turn the waters into blood and to strike the earth with every kind of plague as often as they want.

* **Revelation 11:1** → One day a third Jewish temple will be erected in Jerusalem (not yet built as of the writing of this book). The first temple was built by King Solomon and was destroyed when the Babylonians conquered Israel under the rule of Nebuchadnezzar. The second Jewish temple, built when the Israelites returned from exile, was destroyed in 70 A.D. by a Roman General named Titus. Titus later ruled as the Roman Emperor from 79-81 A.D. The third temple will be built and initially even be supported (under false pretenses) by the man that will one day be revealed as the Antichrist.

* **Revelation 11:2** → The information given to John from Revelation 10:1 through 11:15 creates a pause between the revelation of the sixth and seventh trumpet judgments. During this pause, we are actually taken back in time to the beginning of the seven-year Tribulation period. The two witnesses mentioned in this passage will carry out their ministry during the first 42 months (3.5 years) of the seven-year Tribulation/Great Tribulation period. Let's get a handle on this 42-month period referenced in the last part of Revelation 11:2.

First, it is important to know that there are 360 days in the Jewish prophetic calendar, on which the book of Revelation is based. This equates to 30 days per month. Three and-a-half years equate to 42 months. Therefore, multiplying the number of days gives us the number of days for a 42-month Jewish period = (30 days/month)x (42 months) = 1,260 days.

* **Revelation 11:3** → The two witnesses to whom God grants super powers have the God-given assignment of prophesying (preaching) the truth of God to a godless and rebellious global audience. Keep in mind that all true disciples of Jesus who constituted the church will already have been taken out of the world during the rapture. Many biblical scholars believe these two men are the Old Testament prophets Moses and Elijah. Why? First, the earthly ministries of both of these prophets, beyond proclaiming God's truths, involved performing various miracles of judgment on wicked people and leaders, including both fire [I Kings 18:16-40; II Kings 1:1-19] and plagues [Exodus 7-12]. Secondly, God allowed both Moses and Elijah to appear with Jesus just before he was crucified [Matthew 17:1-9].

Other scholars believe these two witnesses could be Elijah and the apostle John (whom God used to write down the words of the Apocalypse). Why John? Because he was told by the angel in Revelation 10:11, "You must prophesy again about many peoples, nations, languages and kings." John was an elderly man who was exiled by Rome on the island of Patmos when the angel spoke these words to him. While history indicates that John was released from exile and lived his remaining few years of his life in Ephesus, it is not recorded that he fulfilled what was spoken to him by the angel before he died. Thus, some believe that he will fulfill this duty during the 1,260 days of the Tribulation. Only God knows, and that is sufficient.

* **Revelation 11:4-6** → These two witnesses are referred to as olive trees because what will come out of them are words that bring life and refreshment to those who are willing to listen and walk in obedience to God's commands. Throughout history, olive oil has been used for food and cooking, as well as for medicinal and religious purposes. And just as olive trees bear olives that benefit the body, so these men are referred to as olive trees – who will share the life-giving and refreshing fruit of God's eternal

Word. They are referred to as lampstands because they will share the light of life, the Lord Jesus Christ:

> When Jesus spoke again to the people, he said, "I am the light of the world. Whoever follows me will never walk in darkness, but will have the light of life. [John 8:12]

As two of God's specially selected and empowered ambassadors on earth during the Tribulation, they will have the power to emit fire from their mouths and devour those who want to hurt them. In addition, they will have power to control the weather and do other miracles that bring judgment on the wicked and rebellious. Again, all who love fictional superhero characters who fight injustice and evil should be saying, "Wow!" when reading about these real-life super-powered righteous men.

Chapter 22

The Beast of the Abyss

Revelation 11:7-19

MUTANT INSIGHT

Nightcrawler: "Heartless fools; they know not what they do."

[X-Men The Animated Series: Nightcrawler]

People were trying to kill Nightcrawler for no reason other than who they thought he was based on his outward appearance. The word "heartless" is defined as "harsh, unfeeling, or very cruel". The words of Nightcrawler's declaration, "they know not what they do", were pulled from the Bible by the comic writers. The essence of his statement is what Jesus himself said while being crucified. Looking with compassion at those who were spitting on him, mocking him, cursing at him, and killing him with no justification, Jesus said, "Father, forgive them, for they know not what they are doing..." [Luke 23:24]. God's love for us, expressed in his patience, pursuit, and the person of Jesus – who is God incarnate – should cause us to repent (do a 180 degree turn) from our wrong-doing and submit to his love and forgiveness.

The Antichrist Kills, The Christ Resurrects

Revelation 11:7-14

> [7] *Now when they have finished their testimony, the beast that comes up from the Abyss will attack them, and overpower and kill them.* [8] *Their bodies will lie in the street of the great city, which is figuratively called Sodom and Egypt, where also their Lord was crucified.* [9] *For three and a half days men from every people, tribe, language and nation will gaze on their bodies and refuse them burial.* [10] *The inhabitants of the earth will gloat over them and will celebrate by sending each other gifts, because these two prophets had tormented those who live on the earth.* [11] *But after the three and a half days a breath of life from God entered them, and they stood on their feet, and terror struck those who saw them.* [12] *Then they heard a loud voice from heaven saying to them, "Come up here." And they went up to heaven in a cloud, while their enemies looked on.* [13] *At that very hour there was a severe earthquake and a tenth of the city collapsed. Seven thousand people were killed in the earthquake, and the survivors were terrified and gave glory to the God of heaven.* [14] *The second woe has passed; the third woe is coming soon.*

* Revelation 11:7 → Who is the beast that comes from the Abyss? He is none other than the Antichrist. Many Bible teachers and scholars seem to gloss over this beast, either not commenting at all as to who he is or stating that he is the same beast as the one who John sees come out of the sea (Revelation 13). As we continue this study, it will be explained by way of Scripture why I believe the beast out of the Abyss is the Antichrist and not the beast out of the sea. According to the prophecy in Daniel 9:27, he must come before the seven-year Tribulation and Great Tribulation periods begins. How do we know this? Because he will be involved in establishing the future covenant (false peace treaty) between Israel and the surrounding nations that want it destroyed:

> He will confirm a covenant with many for one "seven". In the middle of the "seven" he will put an end to sacrifice and offering. And at the temple he will set up an abomination that causes desolation until the end that is decreed is poured out on him." [Daniel 9:27]

The Antichrist will be on the earth during the 1,260 day time-period when the two witnesses will be administering God's Word and releasing judgments on the earth. At the end of the 3.5 years (Tribulation), he will attack the two witnesses and kill them. The world will rejoice in him and be poised to soon worship him, take his mark (666), and pledge their allegiance to Satan. The reference in Daniel 9:27 to "the abomination that causes desolation" refers to his image that will be worshiped (possibly a statue, 3-D holograph, or some other form). This image will be set up in the third Jewish temple. While the two witnesses are "burdening" the world with God's prophesies, the Antichrist will in contrast make it known that he has come to set the world free from God's rules, restrictions, and commands. He will tell the global population they don't need to repent of sin (sexual perversion, idol worship, witchcraft, and evil of all kinds). On the contrary, he will promote godless living – promoting a "do whatever feels good" philosophy – with Satanism being the foundation. This beast out of the Abyss (Antichrist) will be discussed in more depth in the review of Revelation 13:3 and 17:8-9.

The second series of 42 months that the Bible refers to as the Great Tribulation is first referenced in Revelation 7:14. During the Great Tribulation, the Antichrist will be revealed for who he truly is – the Satan-led world leader who will proclaim himself to be a god and demand to be worshiped in the Third temple. During the Great Tribulation, the Antichrist will lead non-Jews (Gentiles) to overrun and control the Third Temple – until the climatic and awesome second coming of the Lord Jesus Christ.

> Don't let anyone deceive you in any way, for that day will not come until the rebellion occurs and the man of lawlessness is revealed, the man doomed to destruction. He will oppose and will exalt himself over everything that is called God or is worshiped, so that he sets himself up in God's temple, proclaiming himself to be God. [II Thessalonians 2:3-4]

> From the time that the daily sacrifice is abolished and the abomination that causes desolation is set up, there will be 1,290 days. Blessed is the one who waits for and reaches the end of the 1,335 days. [Daniel 12:11-12]

Next, let's get a handle on the two time periods, 1,290 days and 1,335 days mentioned in Daniel 12:11-12 (see the timeline).

```
|---------Tribulation----------|-------- Great Tribulation -------- |
|------- 1,260 days-----|45|30|----------- 1,260 days ----------- |
                      |-------------- 1,290 days ------------- |
                      |-------------- 1,335 days --------------- |
```

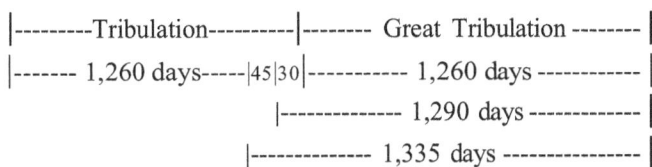

{Timeline spacing is not to scale}

The 1,290 days (see Daniel 12:11) includes the Great Tribulation period plus the preceding 30-day period during which Antichrist abolishes the Jewish daily sacrificial system and sets up the abomination that causes desolation [Revelation 13:14(b)]

The 1,335 days (see Daniel 12:12) includes the 1,290 days plus the 45 preceding days. The 45 days is likely to be the period in which conflict between Antichrist and the Jews begin, leading to the actions listed above.

 * **Revelation 11:8-14** → During this time, Jerusalem will be figuratively called Sodom and Egypt because of the moral decay and idolatry of its inhabitants. The ancient city of Sodom was rebuked by God (and destroyed) because of vile sexual and moral rebellion against God. Ancient Egypt was the seat of idol worship. Revelation 11:8 indicates the two witnesses will be killed in Jerusalem. Revelation 11:10 says the inhabitants of the earth will gloat over their dead bodies and will celebrate by sending each other gifts and partying. Revelation 11:11-13 remind us, however, that it is not wise to gloat against God, his plans, and His people. The millions upon millions who rejoice about the two dead witnesses of God will quake in their boots when they see these two men rise from the dead and then hear

the loud voice from heaven. As they will watch these two men soar into the sky toward heaven, whether in person or through any one of the electronic media methods by which global events can be viewed, they will begin to contemplate what will happen next. Within an hour, they will know – after a severe earthquake strikes and kills 7,000 people.

The Seventh Trumpet Brings Praise In Heaven

Revelation 11:15-19

[15] *The seventh angel sounded his trumpet, and there were loud voices in heaven, which said: "The kingdom of the world has become the kingdom of our Lord and of his Christ, and he will reign for ever and ever."* [16] *And the twenty-four elders, who were seated on their thrones before God, fell on their faces and worshiped God,* [17] *saying: "We give thanks to you, Lord God Almighty, the One who is and who was, because you have taken your great power and have begun to reign.* [18] *The nations were angry; and your wrath has come. The time has come for judging the dead, and for rewarding your servants the prophets and your saints and those who reverence your name, both small and great— and for destroying those who destroy the earth."* [19] *Then God's temple in heaven was opened, and within his temple was seen the ark of his covenant. And there came flashes of lightning, rumblings, peals of thunder, an earthquake and a great hailstorm.*

* **Revelation 11:15-19** → The seventh trumpet is sounded and signals a turning point in the book of Revelation. Jesus the King of kings and Lord of lords shall be glorified! Re-read the words of verses 17-18 and examine your life to determine if you are reconciled to God through Jesus the Savior. If not (or you are not sure), you can turn to God right now in repentance (a spiritual U-turn) and receive the free offer of the forgiveness of sins and a reconciled relationship. The following prayer of repentance can be used as a guide for your own prayer:

> Almighty God, I come to you in the name of Jesus. I acknowledge to you that I am a sinner and I am sorry for my sins and the life that I have lived; I need your forgiveness. I believe that your only begotten Son Jesus Christ shed His precious blood on the cross, dying for my sins and I now turn from my sin and self-directed life. You said in Your Holy Word, Romans 10:9, that if we confess the Lord our God and believe in our hearts that God raised Jesus from the dead, we shall be saved. Right now, I confess Jesus as the Lord of my soul. With my heart, I believe that you, God the Father raised Jesus, God the Son, from the dead. I accept Jesus Christ as my own personal Savior and thank you that, according to your, Word, right now I am saved – forever. Thank you, Jesus, for your unlimited grace which has saved me from my sins. I thank you Jesus that when I stumble along the way, your grace will lead me to repentance [I John 1:7,9]. Lord Jesus, transform my life [Romans 12:1-2] so that I may bring glory and honor to you alone and not to myself. Thank you, Jesus, for dying for me and giving me eternal life. Amen.

MUTANT INSIGHT

Apocalypse: "There's no freedom from me…only freedom through me!"

[X-Men The Animated Series: Obsession]

Apocalypse's bravado and self-exaltation as one who liberates others are hollow words. Not only does he aim to deceive others into falling into his traps of bondage and death, he has fallen victim to the snares of self-deception. He thinks he's all that – when he's not. Many people today have the same outward ego-complex and inner inferiority complex. In the Bible, Psalm 139:7-12 reads as follows:

> Where can I go from your Spirit? Where can I flee from your presence? If I go up to the heavens, you are there; if I make my bed in the depths, you are there. If I rise on the wings of the dawn, if I settle on the far side of the sea, even there your hand will guide me, your right hand will hold me fast. If I say, 'Surely the darkness will hide me and the light become night around me,' even the darkness will not be dark to you; the night will shine like the day, for darkness is as light to you.

The passage above informs readers that it is impossible to escape the presence and dominion of God. He owns the entire universe, including you and me. True freedom – expressed as forgiveness of sins and peace with God, along with the inner-peace, joy, contentment he offers – are gifts granted to us when we yield our lives the Master of all. Like wily mutants who were directionless and off-kilter in life before submitting to Professor X's mentorship and leading, no one will find what they are looking for outside of what God offers.

Chapter 23

Heavenly Signs and Earthly Realities

Revelation 12:1-6

Apocalypse: " I know more of this world than you can even dream…that is why I must destroy it."

[X-Men The Animated Series: The Cure]

Apocalypse's credo, "Only the Strong Will Survive", conforms to the basic premise of Darwinian evolutionary theory – as a way of describing the process of natural selection (or survival of the fittest). His statement above refers to the weakness of both humans and mutants that he's seen over the centuries – as related to their physical and mental strength. His definition has nothing to do with weakness of character, morality and ethics. Like a big bully, his only focus is on who can dominate others.

Unlike the erroneous apocalyptic messages propagated throughout the centuries, God's revelation (apocalypse) of what is to come, though it includes impending judgment on mankind, is not about him being a mean and spiteful God. No, God came in the form of a man over two thousand years ago to die a sacrificial death for mankind so that He might provide forgiveness of sins for all. Jesus referred to Himself as humble and meek [Matthew 11:29]. Meekness is best defined as power under control. He will not destroy the world. He will, however, eradicate sin from the

165

earth and refashion both earth and the heavens. He doesn't look at what man looks at; he looks at the heart (the inner-self) of man.

The Savior's Birth and Protection of Israel

Revelation 12:1-6

> [1] *A great and wondrous sign appeared in heaven: a woman clothed with the sun, with the moon under her feet and a crown of twelve stars on her head.* [2] *She was pregnant and cried out in pain as she was about to give birth.* [3] *Then another sign appeared in heaven: an enormous red dragon with seven heads and ten horns and seven crowns on his heads.* [4] *His tail swept a third of the stars out of the sky and flung them to the earth. The dragon stood in front of the woman who was about to give birth, so that he might devour her child the moment it was born.* [5] *She gave birth to a son, a male child, who will rule all the nations with an iron scepter. And her child was snatched up to God and to his throne.* [6] *The woman fled into the desert to a place prepared for her by God, where she might be taken care of for 1,260 days.*

* **Revelation 12:1** → John sees two great signs in heaven, beginning with the one described in Revelation 12:1-2. We'll read more about the second sign in verse three of this chapter (the enormous red dragon) when chapter fifteen is explored. The woman in this verse represents Israel—hence, the use of the word "sign". The twelve stars in the crown represent the twelve tribes of Jacob (to whom God gave the name "Israel"). The twelve sons (and subsequent tribes) of Jacob were first pictured as stars in a prophetic dream of Joseph (one of Jacob's sons) with Jacob and his wife (Rachel; Joseph's mother) being symbolized by the sun and moon, respectively:

> Then he had another dream, and he told it to his brothers. "Listen," he said, "I had another dream, and this time the sun and moon and eleven stars were bowing down to me." [Genesis 37:9]

As a reminder, Revelation 12 introduces the beginning of the second 3.5 year period called the Great Tribulation. This will be a time in the history of nations when Israel will be hated more than ever before.

* **Revelation 12:2** → The Messiah, Christ Jesus, was born of a virgin from the direct genetic bloodline of Israel (the new name that God gave to Jacob). The prophet Isaiah wrote the following words about 700 years before Jesus' birth:

> For to us a child is born, to us a son is given, and the government will be on his shoulders. And he will be called Wonderful Counselor, Mighty God, Everlasting Father, Prince of Peace. Of the greatness of his government and peace there will be no end. He will reign on David's throne and over his kingdom, establishing and upholding it with justice and righteousness from that time on and forever. The zeal of the LORD Almighty will accomplish this. [Isaiah 9:6-7]

* **Revelation 12:3-4** → This red dragon is Satan. Now you know the Bible verse that has been used as the basis for beginning to portray Satan as a red-horned dragon with a long tail. Note, however, that the red dragon is only a sign. Satan does

not actually look like this. In addition to the judgments of God being poured out on wicked man, Satan will bring terror to the Earth during the Great Tribulation. The dragon pictured here has seven heads and ten horns. The details of these heads and horns will be explained in greater detail when we review Revelation 17:10-12. One third of the angels of heaven joined Satan in the heavenly rebellion against the Lord [Ezekiel 28]. The imagery of the Dragon standing in front of the pregnant woman signifies how Satan tried, by way of King Herod, to prevent the Savior's birth [read Matthew 2:1-20]. Obviously, his plans failed – and always will when it comes to God's sovereign rule.

* **Revelation 12:5** → The male child with the iron scepter is Jesus Christ, the Messiah. In Psalm 2:9, the Messiah (the Anointed One) is pictured ruling the earth with a rod of iron. Ever since God told Satan (the Dragon) in the Garden of Eden [Genesis 3:15] that one day the seed of the woman (who is Christ, by virgin birth since men, not women, have seed) would crush his head, Satan has attempted to prevent the Savior's birth. He has tried this in many ways over the centuries, such as motivating ungodly nations to attack the nation of Israel, leading Israel to abandon God's plan by way of idol (demon) worship, and killing mass numbers of Hebrew baby boys [Exodus 1:8-22 and Matthew 2:1-18]. The last sentence in this verse refers to Christ ascending into heaven after his resurrection, then sitting back down on God's throne in glory – the same eternal position as part of the Triune Godhead that he has had for all eternity.

* **Revelation 12:6** → During this period that launches the Great Tribulation, a portion of Israel's population who will turn to God in repentance and surrender to the Lordship of Jesus. They will be protected from Satan for 1,260 days (3.5 years, the second half of the seven-year period of tribulation). Zechariah 13:8 informs us that two-thirds of Israel will be destroyed during this time but one-third will survive.

Chapter 24

The Great Dragon Hurled Down

Revelation 12:7-12

Cable (speaking about Apocalypse): "…He's pure evil, and that's why he's gotta go!"

[X-Men The Animated Series: Beyond Good and Evil (Part 3)]

Evil is defined as the opposite or absence of good. In every context of life, the battle of good versus evil is evident. In all superhero action movies and comic books, these two forces are pitted against each other. Every year, millions of people around the globe spend considerable amounts of time and money to watch these movies. They applaud heroes who fight against evil forces to protect the innocent, restore justice, and put away the bad guys. In reality, there is a being who is the essence of evil, referred to in the Bible as the father of lies [John 8:44], the prince of the powers of the air [Ephesians 2:2], and the great Dragon. Satan is real and will one day be done away with to the glory of God.

Satan's Ejection from Heaven

Revelation 12:7-12

[7] *And there was war in heaven. Michael and his angels fought against the dragon, and the dragon and his angels fought back.* [8] *But he was not strong enough, and they lost their place in heaven.* [9] *The great dragon was hurled down—that ancient serpent called the devil, or Satan, who leads the whole world astray. He was hurled to the earth, and his angels with him.* [10] *Then I heard a loud voice in heaven say: "Now have come the salvation and the power and the kingdom of our God, and the authority of his Christ. For the accuser of our brothers, who accuses them before our God day and night, has been hurled down.* [11] *They overcame him by the blood of the Lamb and by the word of their testimony; they did not love their lives so much as to shrink from death.* [12] *Therefore rejoice, you heavens and you who dwell in them! But woe to the earth and the sea, because the devil has gone down to you! He is filled with fury, because he knows that his time is short."*

* **Revelation 12:7-9** → The angel Michael is mentioned five times in the Bible (Daniel 10:13,21 12:1, Jude 1:9, Revelation 12:7). According to Daniel 12:1, he is a defender of the people of Israel. He is called "arch" (or chief) angel in Jude 1:9. The role that Michael plays in Daniel 12:1 gives us additional insight into the events taking place in Revelation chapter 12, the Great Tribulation:

At that time Michael shall stand up, the great prince who stands watch over the sons of your people; And there shall be a time of trouble, such as never was since there was a nation, even to that time. And at that time your people shall be delivered, every one who is found written in the book.

At this future point in time, the power of Satan and his angels will be severely restricted. They will no longer have access to the heavenly realm. Their time will now be limited to the final 3.5 years of the seven-year Tribulation period.

MUTANT INSIGHT

Apocalypse: "Behold mutant, you dare challenge Apocalypse – again? Blasphemer, you defile my sacred chamber?"

[X-Men The Animated Series:
Beyond Good and Evil (Part 1): The End of Time]

Blasphemy is defined as the act of insulting God or showing a lack of reverence for him and what He has deemed as holy things. The irony in Apocalypse's statement is that neither he nor his ideals are sacred – that is, reflecting the ideals of God and righteousness. Jesus once had to rebuke people who were pretending to be religious, but were in fact greedy and all about their self-gain. You can read about his response in John 2:13-17 (hint: it involved a whip and him flipping over tables, a foreshadowing of how he will eventually deal with all blasphemers).

* Revelation 12:10-12 → Since the time of mankind's fall from a sinless state (in the garden of Eden after having given in to Satan's temptation) up until the future period laid out in these verses of Revelation, Satan has had access to the throne of God in order to accuse humanity. This is evidenced in the Old Testament when Satan went before the throne of God to accuse a man named Job [Job 1:2,6-10]:

> In the land of Uz there lived a man whose name was Job. This man was blameless and upright; he feared God and shunned evil…One day the angels came to present themselves before the LORD, and Satan also came with them. Then the LORD said to Satan, 'Have you considered my servant Job? There is no one on earth like him; he is blameless and upright, a man who fears God and shuns evil.' 'Does Job fear God for nothing?' Satan replied. 'Have you not put a hedge around him and his household and everything he has? You have blessed the work of his hands, so that his flocks and herds are spread throughout the land. But now stretch out your hand and strike everything he has, and he will surely curse you to your face.' The LORD said to Satan, 'Very well, then, everything he has is in your power, but on the man himself do not lay a finger.' Then Satan went out from the presence of the LORD.

Job's story reveals that until the future time comes when Satan will be hurled down to earth from the heavenly realm [Revelation 12:10], he still has access to the throne of God to accuse the saints (all people who have trusted Christ Jesus as Savior and Lord). That means he's still currently doing this accusing, as a wicked prosecutor. However, all true believers have Jesus, the Lord of the Universe, as their most holy and perfect defense attorney.

During the Great Tribulation, Satan and his demons will become earthbound and confined to this region (earthly dimension). They will no longer have access to heavenly dimensions and the throne of God. They will know that their time to deceive the nations is limited and their judgment is soon coming. The voice in heaven (verses ten and eleven) proclaims the three keys to a victorious Christian life:

1.   **The word of their testimony:** The saints (believers/disciples) who are victorious in the Great Tribulation will boldly proclaim the gospel (truth of Jesus), in both word and uncompromised living, to the Satanically influenced world. [II Timothy 1:7-8];

2.   **The willingness to lay down their lives:** True disciples of Jesus do not love their temporal earthy lives so much as to surrender their eternal lives.

3.   **The rejection of what this world offers:** True and victorious believers in Jesus would never abandon their commitment to him for the sake of temporary gain and/or pleasure. What the world offers is often hollow, fleeting, and ungodly. The focus of Christ-followers should be on eternity and how to glorify the Lord while on this earth. In the Great Tribulation, people will be given a choice: bow to Satan and live or bow down to Jesus and risk losing their lives on the earth. Victorious followers of Christ (saints) will choose death in this world and life forever with Christ.

Chapter 25

Escaping the Dragon

Revelation 12:13-17

Beast: "If, indeed, Apocalypse is the personification of evil, it may be impossible to destroy him."
Cable: "Why?"
Beast: "The conflict between good and evil is part of the fabric of existence. Perhaps the world cannot exist without evil. If Apocalypse is destroyed, evil may only take on another form."

[X-Men The Animated Series: Beyond Good and Evil (Part 3)]

B east's hypothesis about evil's role in the world, supposed- ly balancing the fabric of existence itself, is not accurate in the comic world. Neither is it true in the real world. While evil is undoubtedly part of the fabric of our current existence, God originally created the world without evil's presence [Genesis 1-2; the Garden of Eden]. While Satan has interrupted things with his deceptions, the Lord will one day soon banish him, along with all of his forces of wickedness, from the world for all eternity. Then God will restore his creation without the presence and power of evil. The fabric of existence will be restored to its original beauty and unmarred by the presence and ramifications of sin. We'll dive into this deeper when we review Revelation 20.

Escaping the Dragon

Revelation 12:13-17

> [13] *When the dragon saw that he had been hurled to the earth, he pursued the woman who had given birth to the male child.* [14] *The woman was given the two wings of a great eagle, so that she might fly to the place prepared for her in the desert, where she would be taken care of for a time, times and half a time, out of the serpent's reach.* [15] *Then from his mouth the serpent spewed water like a river, to overtake the woman and sweep her away with the torrent.* [16] *But the earth helped the woman by opening its mouth and swallowing the river that the dragon had spewed out of his mouth.* [17] *Then the dragon was enraged at the woman and went off to make war against the rest of her offspring—those who obey God's commandments and hold to the testimony of Jesus.*

* **Revelation 12:13** → Satan will be confined to the earth during the second half of the Tribulation and begin to escalate his unprecedented persecution of Israel and followers of Jesus. The male child referred to in this verse is the Messiah (Christ) who was caught up to heaven (after his resurrection from the dead) to rule the nations from God's throne. Satan considers the promises made to Israel by God and thinks that by destroying Israel he can prevent his judgment and destruction by God our Savior. Jesus declared before His crucifixion that he would not return until Israel acknowledged Him as their Messiah [read Matthew 23:37-39].

* **Revelation 12:14** → God will protect the woman (Israel) in a sovereign way during the Great Tribulation, both from his judgments being poured out on wicked humanity and from the wrath of the Antichrist that will be unleashed on all who won't bow down to him and Satan. One possible interpretation of the wings of a great eagle that John is describing could be planes taking Jews away in a mass exodus. Refer back to the timeline given in our discussion of Revelation 11:2. The Jews' sacrificial system will be hijacked by the Antichrist seventy-five days before the Great Tribulation begins, giving the Jews almost two and-a-half months to flee. Many Bible scholars believe these Jews will flee to the ancient city of Petra, located in the southern part of Jordan (ancient Edom), famous as a rock-cut city with a water conduit system.

> He [Antichrist] will also invade the Beautiful Land.
> Many countries will fall, but Edom, Moab and the
> leaders of Ammon will be delivered from his hand.
> [Daniel 11:41]

About Petra, "History tells us that the Nabataeans were nomads, dwelling in tents in the desert. Yet, within a few short years they built spectacular and awe inspiring monuments. The magnificent city of Petra is so impressive, that even today tourists stare in awe at the great ruins...this impressive city was hidden away in a cleft in the rock with access through a narrow crack in a mountain. The crack is over 1,200 meters long and 3 to 6 meters wide, flanked by 100-meter high canyon walls."[10] The fleeing Jews will be protected there (and/or some other places) by God during the three and-a-half years of the Great Tribulation.

* **Revelation 12:15-16** → Satan will try to eradicate the fleeing Jews with some sort of flood, but God will provide protection... He always does! As the prophet Isaiah once proclaimed,

> When enemies come in like a flood, the Spirit of the
> Lord will put them to flight. [Isaiah 59:19]

* **Revelation 12:17** → The Dragon, who will control much of the world's economic, political, and world religious systems by means of the Antichrist (incarnated by Satan), is enraged because he failed to destroy Israel. His anger will now be unleashed against all who are associated with the God of Israel. In Revelation chapter thirteen, Satan puts together a plan to separate all who might have an allegiance to any but him. He makes war with the rest of the women's offspring – all those who know Christ are to be hunted down, forced to recant (if captured) or be killed.

Chapter 26

The Dragon and His Two Beasts

Revelation 13:1-10

Apocalypse: "You serve me well Mystique. Such loyalty will be rewarded. The rest shall be my slaves."

[X-Men The Animated Series: Come the Apocalypse]

S ervants of Apocalypse must always be looking over their shoulders, wondering if his, "Only the Strong Will Survive" philosophy will make them the next target of his folly and cleansing trials. Loyalty to Apocalypse does not mean loyalty from him. Slaves are meant to serve. When deemed no longer strong enough to accomplish their assigned tasks, they are discarded for more suitable replacements.

Satan, the real adversary of our souls, endeavors to deceive us for the purpose of seeing us bound in slavery and missing the freedom the God offers us in Jesus. In contrast, the Lord enslaves no one, for He has no need of slaves. The remarkable truth is that while we were created to serve God, he Himself chose to become a servant by coming into the world to lay down His life sacrificially as our sin-bearer and Savior.

Explosion of Satan Worship

Revelation 13:1-10

¹ *And the dragon stood on the shore of the sea. And I saw a beast coming out of the sea. He had ten horns and seven heads, with ten crowns on his horns, and on each head a blasphemous name.* ² *The beast I saw resembled a leopard, but had feet like those of a bear and a mouth like that of a lion. The dragon gave the beast his power and his throne and great authority.* ³ *One of the heads of the beast seemed to have had a fatal wound, but the fatal wound had been healed. The whole world was astonished and followed the beast.* ⁴ *Men worshiped the dragon because he had given authority to the beast, and they also worshiped the beast and asked, "Who is like the beast? Who can make war against him?"* ⁵ *The beast was given a mouth to utter proud words and blasphemies and to exercise his authority for forty-two months.* ⁶ *He opened his mouth to blaspheme God, and to slander his name and his dwelling place and those who live in heaven.* ⁷ *He was given power to make war against the saints and to conquer them. And he was given authority over every tribe, people, language and nation.* ⁸ *All inhabitants of the earth will worship the beast—all whose names have not been written in the book of life belonging to the Lamb that was slain from the creation of the world.* ⁹ *He who has an ear, let him hear.* ¹⁰ *If anyone is to go into captivity, into captivity he will go. If anyone is to be killed with the sword, with the sword he will be killed. This*

calls for patient endurance and faithfulness on the part of the saints.

* **Revelation 13:1(a)** → As we have just read, Satan will be cast to Earth at the end of the Tribulation (first 42 months = 1,260 days = 3.5 years). Knowing that his time is short before being judged, he will ramp up his deception in the world like never before. This deception will be carried out by the Antichrist (the beast that comes from the Abyss) and the other beast, the False Prophet, that comes out of the earth (we'll learn about him in Revelation 13:11). Thus, Satan creates an unholy "trinity", with himself as the boss, the Antichrist as the political and economic leader, and the False Prophet as the religious leader.

* **Revelation 13:1(b)** → The seven-headed beast that John saw coming out of the sea is a beast of nations and represents the seven dominant kingdoms that ruled the majority of the known world during various times throughout history *and* who have had direct impact (socially, economically, politically, and spiritually) on the nation of Israel. While there have been other world empires that have ruled throughout history, they did not have a direct bearing on Israel. Thus, they are not included in this prophecy. The seven heads of the beast represent the kings of these seven kingdoms which will be revived as global powers in the future – all in alliance as a single "beast" under the control of Satan (the Dragon).

> This calls for a mind with wisdom. The seven heads are seven hills on which the woman sits [not the woman of chapter twelve verse one (Israel); rather, it is the woman of chapter seventeen]. They are also seven kings. Five have fallen, one is, the other has not yet come; but when he does come, he must remain for only a little while. The beast who once was, and now is not, is an eighth king. He belongs to the

seven and is going to his destruction. "The ten horns you saw are ten kings who have not yet received a kingdom, but who for one hour will receive authority as kings along with the beast. They have one purpose and will give their power and authority to the beast. They will wage war against the Lamb, but the Lamb will triumph over them because he is Lord of lords and King of kings—and with him will be his called, chosen and faithful followers. [Revelation 17:9-14]

So now let's discover which seven nations are being referenced as the seven heads of the beast, specifically stated as "five have fallen, one is, the other has not yet come."

The "five have fallen" nations that had already fallen at the time John wrote down Revelation are, in chronological order, Egypt, Assyria, Babylon, Media-Persia, and Greece. The nation in power during John's writing of Revelation, of which he referred to as "one is", was Rome, or the Roman Empire. The nation that "has not yet come" is the end-times nation, or federation of nations, referred to by many biblical-prophecy scholars as the future Revived Roman Empire.

This future empire will be headed one day by the Antichrist. He will be the eighth king [Revelation 17:11], the one whom the angel tells John is "the other has yet to come", referred to as "the beast who comes from the Abyss" [Revelation 11:7]. The ten horns and ten crowns refer to the ten rulers and the ten-nations that will subject themselves to the authority and rule of the seventh king (the beast out of the Abyss, referred to as the Antichrist).

For fascinating reading about how God foretold through his prophets the emergence of the kingdoms listed above, read Daniel 2, 7, and 8. In Daniel 2, the king of Babylon (Nebuchadnezzar) saw in a dream

...an enormous, dazzling statue, awesome in appearance. The head of the statue was made of pure gold, its chest and arms of silver, its belly and thighs of bronze, its legs of iron, its feet partly of iron and partly of baked clay. [Daniel 2:32-33]

The prophet Daniel not only told Nebuchadnezzar what he saw in his dream, but also interpreted the dream for the king:

You are that head of gold. After you, another kingdom will arise, inferior to yours. Next, a third kingdom, one of bronze, will rule over the whole earth. Finally, there will be a fourth kingdom, strong as iron—for iron breaks and smashes everything—and as iron breaks things to pieces, so it will crush and break all the others. Just as you saw that the feet and toes were partly of baked clay and partly of iron, so this will be a divided kingdom; yet it will have some of the strength of iron in it, even as you saw iron mixed with clay. As the toes were partly iron and partly clay, so this kingdom will be partly strong and partly brittle. And just as you saw the iron mixed with baked clay, so the people will be a mixture and will not remain united, any more than iron mixes with clay. [Daniel 2:38(b)-43]

Daniel had further visions and was told by the angel Gabriel that the kingdom of Babylon would be overthrown by Media and Persia and they, in turn, would be overthrown by Greece (Alexander the Great). Each of these prophecies came to pass exactly as God's Word predicted.

* **Revelation 13:2(a)** → John's reference to how the seven-headed beast had characteristics like a leopard, bear, and lion are

consistent with Daniel's vision, which took place about 690 years before John's:

> Daniel said: "In my vision at night I looked, and there before me were the four winds of heaven churning up the great sea. Four great beasts, each different from the others, came up out of the sea. The first was like a lion, and it had the wings of an eagle. I watched until its wings were torn off and it was lifted from the ground so that it stood on two feet like a human being, and the mind of a human was given to it. And there before me was a second beast, which looked like a bear. It was raised up on one of its sides, and it had three ribs in its mouth between its teeth. It was told, "Get up and eat your fill of flesh!" After that, I looked, and there before me was another beast, one that looked like a leopard. And on its back it had four wings like those of a bird. This beast had four heads, and it was given authority to rule. [Dan. 7:2-6]

* Revelation 13:2(b) → Most of us have seen television shows and movies that have multi-plot scenes and various characters that may seem disconnected but, in fact, are all linked to the same goal, plan, or outcome. Such is the case with this beast of nations. Each of these kingdoms and their kings are linked with the same characteristics: world-domination, immorality, bloodshed (including persecution of Jews), and the worship of idols and kings – all led and empowered by the Dragon, Satan. He has always desired to be worshiped like God. He even had the audacity to ask Jesus to bow down to him in exchange for the chance to rule as a king:

Again, the devil took him to a very high mountain and showed him all the kingdoms of the world and their splendor. "All this I will give you," he said, "if you will bow down and worship me." Jesus said to him, "Away from me, Satan! For it is written: 'Worship the Lord your God, and serve him only.'"" [Matthew 4:8-10]

* **Revelation 13:3** → One of the seven heads (a king) of the beast that comes out of the sea (the ten-nation federation ruled by Satan) will be come to power only for a little while. He is the seventh head of the dragon and will remain in power for a little while – to be superseded by the eight king (Antichrist), as revealed in Revelation 17:9-11. Antichrist (the eighth king who will come from the 7th) is referred to in Revelation 11:7 as the beast that comes out of the Abyss. Most respected Bible scholars teach that the Antichrist will be born in the era in which he will rise to power, be fatally killed, and then be healed and come back to life. There may be another option to consider. The remarkable fact about him is that the Bible says that this beast that comes from the Abyss. Is this a former world-famous despot who was killed in the past and who's soul, in spiritual form, was cast into the Abyss (not Hades) to be held for this future time in history? That's what the Scripture seems to state. If so, his body and soul were cast into this place sometime in the past, prior to John seeing the visions, hearing the words, and writing the words of this prophetic book. In the Abyss he will be allowed to heal from his fatal wound and live without aging until he is brought back to earth from the Abyss. The world will be astonished by his reappearance (seeming resurrection from the dead) and follow this Satan-empowered man.

* **Revelation 13:4-10** → Satan, portrayed in chapter twelve as a seven-headed dragon, will be cast out of heaven and will be the source of power and authority of the seven-headed beast (Revived

Roman Empire) that arises from the sea. He will be worshiped by all people who reject God, whose names are not written on the Lamb's (Jesus) book of life. These people will also worship the Antichrist, who will curse God, heaven, and all who are there. They will deliberately ignore God and blaspheme the name of Jesus to their eternal woe [Revelation 13:5-6]. If you missed the key point, let me reiterate it: The world, rejecting Christ, will openly worship Satan. God's judgment is appropriate.

MUTANT INSIGHT

Nightcrawler: "Hold me in the light of God. Protect me from danger. Save me by your command. Listen to my prayer and keep me safe."

[X-Men: Apocalypse]

Trapped in a helicopter along with other X-Men, flying to an unknown destination, Nightcrawler prays to the Lord during a time of fear, uncertainty, and danger. Those who are wise should do the same. Why? Because God loves us and encourages us to seek Him with a sincere and earnest heart. The essence of the prayer above can be found in Psalms 16 and 71; check them out.

Chapter 27

The Mark of the Beast

Revelation 13:11-18

Apocalypse: "Do what you will, for I fear no one."

[X-Men The Animated Series: Beyond Good and Evil Part 4]

E vildoers often speak with great bravado. We see this character trait (pride) in all comic villains. Their boasting of having neither fear of authority nor respect of the rule of law point to their deep insecurities, poor character development, and deceptive philosophies that are anti-God. The Bible says about people like this, "Fools find no pleasure in understanding, but delight in airing their own opinions." [Proverbs 18:2]

Revelation 13 reveals three anti-God beings, Satan and the two beasts, who blaspheme God, make murderous threats against God's followers, and appear to have no fear. The key word is "appear". In actuality, Satan and demons show the Lord reverence when they come before him, like a scared criminal before a judge in a court [read Matthew 8:29 and James 2:19]. Satan and demons know their end. They want to deceive the nations so that myriad people from across the globe will share their fate.

666 – The Mark of the Beast

Revelation 13:11-18

 [11] *Then I saw another beast, coming out of the earth. He had two horns like a lamb, but he spoke like a dragon.* [12] *He exercised all the authority of the first beast on his behalf, and made the earth and its inhabitants worship the first beast, whose fatal wound had been healed.* [13] *And he performed great and miraculous signs, even causing fire to come down from heaven to earth in full view of men.* [14] *Because of the signs he was given power to do on behalf of the first beast, he deceived the inhabitants of the earth. He ordered them to set up an image in honor of the beast who was wounded by the sword and yet lived.* [15] *He was given power to give breath to the image of the first beast, so that it could speak and cause all who refused to worship the image to be killed.* [16] *He also forced everyone, small and great, rich and poor, free and slave, to receive a mark on his right hand or on his forehead,* [17] *so that no one could buy or sell unless he had the mark, which is the name of the beast or the number of his name.* [18] *This calls for wisdom. If anyone has insight, let him calculate the number of the beast, for it is man's number. His number is 666.*

* **Revelation 13:11-18** → The second beast is the Antichrist's False Prophet, a man of deception and destruction. While Antichrist will be the political and economic leader, the False Prophet will be the spiritual leader, leading the earth's inhabitants astray by way of satanic deception. He will perform great signs and counterfeit wonders in the name of the Antichrist. Keep in mind that Satan *always* distorts the truth of God. Thus, he will create his own demented "trinity", consisting of himself, the Antichrist, and the second beast (False Prophet).

An image of the Antichrist will be the focus of worldwide worship. All who refuse to worship this beast or his image will be killed. The False Prophet will most likely be the leader of the world-wide religion in the second half of the Tribulation period (Great Tribulation), during which the saints (all followers of Christ) will be persecuted. In order to enforce this worldwide religion of the second beast, an economic system will be established demanding total submission to Antichrist. Those who refuse will be killed or cutoff from society. They will be unable to buy or sell without total submission [see 13:16-18]. Later, this world-wide, demonically-led religion will be minimized, if not eradicated [Revelation 17:15-17] as the Beast and Satan become the focus of worship.

MUTANT INSIGHT

Apocalypse: *"She (Rogue) has great powers. We'll use the machine [to] make her my slave."*

[X-Men The Animated Series: The Cure]

All villains prey on weaker people. They also target others whom they may wish to recruit in order to advance their own cause. While such villains promise great rewards to those who follow them, the end-result of linking with them is destructive living, bondage and possibly death. This is how Apocalypse operates.

Moving beyond the world of fiction, *the* villain of all villains is Satan. He desires to deceive as many people as he can into rejecting God and his offer of love, forgiveness of sin, and the promise of eternal life. Satan's goal is to enslave people to sin in this life and see them doomed to hell for eternity. Consider these words from Romans 6:16,

> Don't you know that when you offer yourselves to someone as obedient slaves, you are slaves of the one you obey—whether you are slaves to sin, which leads to death, or to obedience, which leads to righteousness?

Now, listen to the liberating words of Jesus,

> Very truly I tell you, everyone who sins is a slave to sin. Now a slave has no permanent place in the family, but a son belongs to it forever. So if the Son sets you free, you will be free indeed. [John 8:34-36]

Chapter 28

Songs, Shouts, Smoke, and A Sickle

Revelation 14:1-20

Nightcrawler: "Your presence here was a great blessing."
Wolverine: "What'd ya' mean blessing? Look at this place; we blew it!
Nightcrawler: "I disagree. Brother Reinhart understands his tragic mistake and has repented. The townspeople no longer look at me with fear in their hearts. There was no loss of life. All are reasons to be thankful.
Rouge: "What about the monastery?"
Nightcrawler: "A great tragedy. But it was only stone and mortar. The foundation that God has built in our hearts can never be destroyed."
Wolverine: "Man, I don't get you."
Nightcrawler: "Here (hands Wolverine a Bible), I've marked a few passages you may find rewarding. Remember, Herr Logan, [see with] different eyes."

[X-Men The Animated Series: Nightcrawler]

Like many mutants, Nightcrawler has experienced great hardships in life due to his physical appearance and people's misconceptions of mutants. However, because of God's love for him, Nightcrawler's bitterness, fears, and thoughts of retaliation were overrun by the fruit of God in his life: love, joy, peace, longsuffering, kindness, goodness, faithfulness, goodness, and self-control. His perspective in life was no longer governed by negative emotions and feelings. Rather, he chose to build his life on the immovable foundation of God's unchanging truths and transforming Word (the Bible). He didn't brush over life's hardships and tragedies. Instead, he submitted to God and anchored himself on God's unconditional love.

The Song of Only A Few Good Men

Revelation 14:1-5

> [1] *Then I looked, and there before me was the Lamb, standing on Mount Zion, and with him 144,000 who had his name and his Father's name written on their foreheads.* [2] *And I heard a sound from heaven like the roar of rushing waters and like a loud peal of thunder. The sound I heard was like that of harpists playing their harps.* [3] *And they sang a new song before the throne and before the four living creatures and the elders. No one could learn the song except the 144,000 who had been redeemed from the earth.* [4] *These are those who did not defile themselves with women, for they kept themselves pure. They follow the Lamb wherever he goes. They were purchased from among men and offered as first-fruits to God and the Lamb.* [5] *No lie was found in their mouths; they are blameless.*

* **Revelation 14:1** → John sees the Lamb (Jesus) standing on Mount Zion with the 144,000 specially selected Jewish men

192

about whom we read about in Revelation 7:1-8. Mount Zion is a hill in Jerusalem that has been a place of significant events in the history of Israel and God's unfolding plan of redeeming mankind. Mount Zion is synonymous with Mount Moriah, where Abraham took his son Isaac, in obedience to God, to offer him as a sacrifice [read Genesis 22:1-19]. It is the site where the Jewish Temple was located as well as where King David built the nation of Israel's capital, Jerusalem, also called the "City of David".

* **Revelation 14:2-3** → John heard a loud sound from heaven, like harpists and a choir, along with the 144,000 who are gathered with Jesus, singing a new song. Question: Is there a new song that needs to be sung from your heart? Isn't it time to go to higher levels of commitment and purposeful living for God? He is the source of peace and joy, offering to all the free gift of forgiveness of sins. The Bible says that these 144,000 were redeemed from the earth. So as the second half of the seven-year Tribulation period begins (the Great Tribulation), they are no longer on the earth proclaiming God's message of repentance as they did during the first half of the seven-year Tribulation period. Do you know what the word "redeem" means? This word was the theme of the Ant Man movie, released in America on July 17, 2015.

> **redeem** (verb): to make (something that is bad, unpleasant, etc.) better or more acceptable; to exchange; to buy back; to recover.

Jesus sacrificially laid down his life to redeem all who are willing to submit to his Lordship.

> You see, at just the right time, when we were still powerless, Christ died for the ungodly. Very rarely will anyone die for a righteous person, though for a good person someone might possibly dare to die.

But God demonstrates his own love for us in this: While we were still sinners, Christ died for us. [Romans 5:6-8]

* **Revelation 14:4-5** → With regard to the statement, "not defiled with women", the Bible is not saying that sex, in and of itself, is defilement. No, sex is a wonderful gift that God gave to mankind to be experienced and enjoyed in the way that he planned: marriage between a man and a woman. God created sex, so how could it be a defilement? The mention of sexual defilement refers to what will be going on in the world during the later times. There will be worship of Satan and all kinds of open sensuality, lust, lying and non-committed relationships. These 144,000 men will not be down with that type of living. Because of the urgency of the day and the special call of God on their lives, these men will be single-minded. They don't involve themselves in the concerns of any temporal issues and earthly pleasures – including of marriage and sex – during this intense period of time in which God calls them into service.

Our Deeds Will Follow Us...So Do Good, Be Good

Revelation 14:6-13

> ⁶ *Then I saw another angel flying in midair, and he had the eternal gospel to proclaim to those who live on the earth—to every nation, tribe, language and people.* ⁷ *He said in a loud voice, "Fear God and give him glory, because the hour of his judgment has come. Worship him who made the heavens, the earth, the sea and the springs of water."* ⁸ *A second angel followed and said, "Fallen! Fallen is Babylon the Great, which made all the nations drink the maddening wine of her adul-*

teries." [9] *A third angel followed them and said in a loud voice: "If anyone worships the beast and his image and receives his mark on the forehead or on the hand,* [10] *he, too, will drink of the wine of God's fury, which has been poured full strength into the cup of his wrath. He will be tormented with burning sulfur in the presence of the holy angels and of the Lamb.* [11] *And the smoke of their torment rises forever and ever. There is no rest day or night for those who worship the beast and his image, or for anyone who receives the mark of his name."* [12] *This calls for patient endurance on the part of the saints who obey God's commandments and remain faithful to Jesus.* [13] *Then I heard a voice from heaven say, "Write: Blessed are the dead who die in the Lord from now on." "Yes," says the Spirit, "they will rest from their labor, for their deeds will follow them."*

* **Revelation 14:6-13** → During the church age, the period that is measured from the resurrection of the Lord Jesus Christ until the future event referred to as the rapture, it is the assignment of Christians to share the good news of the kingdom of God and the Lord Jesus Christ. However, after the rapture of the church, God will appoint special envoys to proclaim the message of the kingdom of God, such as the 144,000 Jewish men, the two witnesses [Revelation11:1-14], and even angels, as mentioned in these verses.

Each year, millions of people clamor to see superhero movies, among the highest grossing movies of all times. These movies are all about super-powered humans and other beings who work to fight evil, uphold justice, and redeem people in trouble. Yet, in real life during the Tribulation period, when real-life men with super-powers along with angelic beings (with greater power than fictional characters such Thor) appear, the majority of the world's inhabitants will ignore, reject, and hate these God-ordained and powerful messengers. The same people who applaud fictional heroes for fighting evil will abhor the real-life men and beings that God sends to combat evil. Instead, they will be worshiping Satan and seeking to fulfill their sinful passions.

This is the deception of Satan. The people who will make bold and public decisions to follow Jesus during this future time on earth will be eternally forgiven by God and saved from the penalty of sin. They will spend eternity with God as heirs of his Kingdom. It is also true that most who follow God rather than Satan during this time period will be persecuted, hunted down, and possibly killed. However, their reward will be great. Verse thirteen informs us that their faithful obedience to Jesus will be rewarded forever and ever. The same applies for us today. Be faithful to the Lord!

MUTANT INSIGHT

Apocalypse: "And time, my friends, is the greatest power in existence. Unfortunately for you and your universe, time has run out."

[X-Men The Animated Series: Beyond Good and Evil Part 4]

The words spoken above by Apocalypse, while from a fictional cartoon, align in an uncanny way with the words of holy Scripture that we've read thus far. Time is, indeed, our most precious commodity. Think about it: you can earn $100, spend it (or lose it), then earn another $100. However, no one can earn more minutes to replace those that have elapsed. Once it's gone, that time will never be replaced or seen again.

All of us were born with a shelf life, or "expiration date". God is sovereign and omniscient. He knows when each one of us will breathe our last breath in this life. Hebrews 9:27 says, "And as it is appointed unto men once to die, but after this the judgment". Don't let time run out on you without Jesus Christ as your personal Lord and Savior. Once you get that settled, then share this great news of forgiveness of sins and salvation with others.

The Great Winepress

Revelation 14:14-20

[14] *I looked, and there before me was a white cloud, and seated on the cloud was one "like a son of man" with a crown of gold on his head and a sharp sickle in his hand.* [15] *Then another angel came out of the temple and called in a loud voice to him who was sitting on the cloud, "Take your sickle and reap, because the time to reap has come, for the harvest of the earth is ripe."* [16] *So he who was seated on the cloud swung his sickle over the earth, and the earth was harvested.* [17] *Another angel came out of the temple in heaven, and he too had a sharp sickle.* [18] *Still another angel, who had charge of the fire, came from the altar and called in a loud voice to him who had the sharp sickle, "Take your sharp sickle and gather the clusters of grapes from the earth's vine, because its grapes are ripe."* [19] *The angel swung his sickle on the earth, gathered its grapes and threw*

197

them into the great winepress of God's wrath. [20] *They were trampled in the winepress outside the city, and blood flowed out of the press, rising as high as the horses' bridles for a distance of 1,600 stadia.*

* **Revelation 14:14-20** → Many of the world's armies, from various nations, will one day be gathered to Jerusalem for one last attempt to destroy Israel, as well as Jesus, upon His return to the earth. This battle is referred to as the battle of Armageddon. We will discuss this in more detail when Revelation 16:14-16 is reviewed. At this battle, Jesus will not come as a Lamb, but as a Lion. The prophet Zechariah describes this coming judgment on the nations who converge on Jerusalem. Zechariah 14:12 informs us that,

> And this shall be the plague with which the LORD will strike all the people who fought against Jerusa-lem: Their flesh shall dissolve while they stand on their feet, their eyes shall dissolve in their sockets and their tongues shall dissolve in their mouths.

Again, let us take to heart what we are reading. Jesus is no longer a babe in a manger. No, he is the eternal Savior and Judge. What we are reading is neither a fable nor "possibly" going to happen. No, what we are reading is true and will definitely occur. The apocalypse, the revealing of what was previously hidden or unknown regarding God's plan of redemption during the end-times, has been clearly given to mankind, including you who are reading this book. There are only two options one has when confronted with the truths of the apocalypse. Option one is to act in belief and turn to the Lord Jesus Christ for salvation. Option two is reject Jesus, turn from God to Satan, and experience God's wrath and everlasting punishment. The choice is yours.

Chapter 29

Seven Angels and Seven Plagues

Revelation 15:1-8

Gambit: "Ah, Paris, back in the civilized world!"

Rogue: "I don't know. Those quiet little monks were starting to grow on me.

Gambit: "Face it Cher, those monks kid themselves. We on our own in 'dis world. Life is random; deal you a full house or a busted flush...(Rogue gets up from table and walks away frustrated).. "What'd I say!?"

Rogue: "(Sighs and says to herself) What if he's right? What if there's nuthin else? [then the wind blows a newspaper into her face. She pulls it away to read the headline, "EGLISE RESTOREE", which is translated in English to mean, "Church Restored". Looking up, she sees the church in front of her; she walks in and sees Wolverine on his knees – reading the Bible and praying.]

[X-Men The Animated Series: Nightcrawler]

After teaming with Wolverine and Gambit to help Nightcrawler overcome a community against him, Rogue reflects back on her time at the monastery where Nightcrawler lived, worshiped and served. She states that the humble and godly lives of the monks had caused her defenses towards religion and God to soften. However, Gambit tells her that there is no God and that she must wake up to the fact that she is her best bet for peace, joy, contentment and purpose. As she contemplates the meaning of life and whether there's a loving and sovereign God who loves her, the flyer "randomly" hits her in the face and she is drawn to the church. Going inside of the sanctuary, she sees none other than "Mr. Gruff" himself, Wolverine. She sees a man with the ability to heal from anything on his knees reading the Bible and praying to God. She sees that no one, not even Wolverine, can bring themselves inner-peace, joy, contentment, and purpose. Only God can give us these gifts that will empower us for godly and extraordinary living.

God's Wrath – Nearing Completion

Revelation 15:1-4

> [1] *I saw in heaven another great and marvelous sign: seven angels with the seven last plagues— last, because with them God's wrath is completed.* [2] *And I saw what looked like a sea of glass mixed with fire and, standing beside the sea, those who had been victorious over the beast and his image and over the number of his name. They held harps given them by God* [3] *and sang the song of Moses the servant of God and the song of the Lamb: "Great and marvelous are your deeds, Lord God Almighty. Just and true are your ways, King of the ages.* [4] *Who will not fear you, O Lord, and bring glory to your name? For you alone are holy. All nations will come and worship before you, for your righteous acts have been revealed."*

* **Revelation 15:1** → This is the third sign that John has seen in heaven (the first and second being in Revelation 12:1 and 12:3, respectively). God's wrath will be complete after these seven angels dispense what is given to them in verse seven (the "seven bowl judgments").

* **Revelation 15:2-4** → Chapters 13 and 14 informed us that Satan and his puppet man, the Antichrist (Beast out the Abyss), will consider all who don't bow down to them as weak and dispensable – and will kill them. Revelation 15:2 says, in contrast, that God will consider *victorios* those killed for not worshiping the beast (the Antichrist), his image, and his number. God has promised to reward all who choose to suffer for doing right rather than compromise, sell him out, and do evil. Are you enduring a trial(s) in life right now because of your faith in God and stance for righteousness? If so, be patient and persevere in faith. God knows your struggle and cares for you. Seek him earnestly, do all that you can, need to, and should do – trusting Him for the rest. Remember to view trials and tests in life in life from God's perspective: James 1:2-8:

> Consider it pure joy, my brothers and sisters, when-
> ever you face trials of many kinds, because you know
> that the testing of your faith produces perseverance.
> Let perseverance finish its work so that you may be
> mature and complete, not lacking anything. If any of
> you lacks wisdom, you should ask God, who gives
> generously to all without finding fault, and it will be
> given to you. But when you ask, you must believe
> and not doubt, because the one who doubts is like
> a wave of the sea, blown and tossed by the wind.
> That person should not expect to receive anything
> from the Lord. Such a person is double-minded and
> unstable in all they do.

Seven Angels With Seven Bowls of God's Wrath

Revelation 15:5-8

⁵After this I looked and in heaven the temple, that is, the tabernacle of the Testimony, was opened. ⁶ Out of the temple came the seven angels with the seven plagues. They were dressed in clean, shining linen and wore golden sashes around their chests. ⁷ Then one of the four living creatures gave to the seven angels seven golden bowls filled with the wrath of God, who lives forever and ever. ⁸ And the temple was filled with smoke from the glory of God and from his power, and no one could enter the temple until the seven plagues of the seven angels were completed.

* **Revelation 15:5-8** → In a final act of judgment upon the earth due to mankind's wickedness and rebellion, God's wrath will be poured out on those inhabitants of the world who will choose to reject him and follow Satan. At the completion of the seventh bowl judgment, the Lord Jesus Christ will return to earth with the saints (all who trusted him as Savior and Lord). He will rule on earth for a thousand years (this will be discussed in the review of Revelation 20). After this, he will redo the very nature of the earth and the heavens. Along with a new earth (not a new planet, but, rather, a totally reformatted earth with the presence and ramifications of sin totally removed), he will bring to earth the majestic new city that he has created in heaven, called the New Jerusalem. This will be discussed in the review of Revelation 21.

Truly, no eye has seen and no ear has heard what marvelous, majestic, and eternal wonders God has in store for all who love Him and seek to glorify Him. The choice is ours to either accept him or reject him. Have you made your choice? And let's be clear, passive indifference toward God is just as much a rejection of him as active rebellion.

Chapter 30

God's Wrath Poured Out

Revelation 16:1-11

Magneto: "I never believed you Apocalypse. I am not a fool."
Apocalypse: "Traitors! You dare to attack your master?
Magneto: "I call no one master; especially one who would destroy the innocent along with the guilty!"

[X-Men The Animated Series: Beyond Good and Evil Part 4]

Unlike the stance that Magneto takes in the exchange above with Apocalypse, many real-life people who are thirsty for money, power, and/or fame willingly follow others whom wise people would avoid. Greed and lust dull the senses of those who become ensnared by their luring and deceptive promises. And make no mistake about it, greed and lust do want to become your masters – to take you down for the count and remove you far from the grace and mercy of God. Consider the following admonition:

> Have nothing to do with the fruitless deeds of dark-
> ness, but rather expose them...This is why it is said:
> "Wake up, sleeper, rise from the dead, and Christ
> will shine on you." Be very careful, then, how you
> live—not as unwise but as wise, making the most
> of every opportunity, because the days are evil.

Therefore do not be foolish, but understand what the Lord's will is." [Ephesians 5:11-17]

The Seven Bowls of God's Wrath

Revelation 16:1-7

[1] *Then I heard a loud voice from the temple saying to the seven angels, "Go, pour out the seven bowls of God's wrath on the earth."* [2] *The first angel went and poured out his bowl on the land, and ugly and painful sores broke out on the people who had the mark of the beast and worshiped his image.* [3] *The second angel poured out his bowl on the sea, and it turned into blood like that of a dead man, and every living thing in the sea died.* [4] *The third angel poured out his bowl on the rivers and springs of water, and they became blood.* [5] *Then I heard the angel in charge of the waters say: "You are just in these judgments, you who are and who were, the Holy One, because you have so judged;* [6] *for they have shed the blood of your saints and prophets, and you have given them blood to drink as they deserve."* [7] *And I heard the altar respond: "Yes, Lord God Almighty, true and just are your judgments."*

* **Revelation 16:1** → God's seven bowl judgments stand in contrast to the seven seal and seven trumpet judgments. Unlike the seal and trumpet judgments, the bowl judgments are not meant to move humanity toward repentance with the goal of seeing them reject Satan's deception and make a decision to submit to Christ Jesus. Rather, these judgments have two specific objectives. First, to unleash God's punishment against ungodly rebels who have worshipped Satan, rejoiced in evil, and killed all who did not join them. Second, to make preparation for the triumphal return of the Lord Jesus Christ [II Peter 3:3-14].

> Above all, you must understand that in the last days scoffers will come, scoffing and following their own evil desires. They will say, "Where is this 'coming' he promised? Ever since our ancestors died, everything goes on as it has since the beginning of creation." But they deliberately forget that long ago by God's word the heavens came into being and the earth was formed out of water and by water. By these waters also the world of that time was deluged and destroyed. By the same word the present heavens and earth are reserved for fire, being kept for the day of judgment and destruction of the ungodly. But do not forget this one thing, dear friends: With the Lord a day is like a thousand years, and a thousand years are like a day. The Lord is not slow in keeping his promise, as some understand slowness. Instead he is patient with you, not wanting anyone to perish, but everyone to come to repentance. But the day of the Lord will come like a thief. The heavens will disappear with a roar; the elements will be destroyed by fire, and the earth and everything in it will be laid bare. Since everything will be destroyed in this way, what kind of people ought you to be? You ought to live holy and godly lives as you look forward to the day of God and speed its coming. That day will bring about the destruction of the heavens by fire, and the elements will melt in the heat. But in keeping with his promise we are

looking forward to a new heaven and a new earth,
where righteousness dwells. So then, dear friends,
since you are looking forward to this, make every
effort to be found spotless, blameless and at peace
with him.

The second coming of Jesus will not be like his first coming.
His first coming into the world was marked by a humble birth in
a lowly and obscure setting. His second coming will be marked
by omnipotent power, heavenly glory, and unrivaled majesty.
The first coming culminated with Jesus being deliberately killed
by men. The second coming will culminate in Jesus battling and
killing his enemies. Yes, he is the God of peace; but woe unto
those who reject him. The scene of Revelation 16 occurs after the
inhabitants of the world have been given a final choice to either
(1) receive the mark of the Beast (Antichrist), worship Satan, and
live or (2) refuse the mark, place their faith in Jesus and, most
likely die – as discussed in chapter fifteen.

Sadly, and to their eternal doom, most on earth make the
decision to receive the mark of the beast. Some will do this out of
fear of death at the hands of Antichrist. Most, however, will take
the mark because of their hatred of God. Conversely, others will
choose to trust God and not renounce their faith in Jesus Christ
even in the face of death. Some others who place their faith
in Christ will live in hiding. After the earth's inhabitants have
made their clear choice of defiance against God, He begins the
judgments of wrath by commanding the angels to pour out the
bowls on the earth.

* **Revelation 16:2** → Inhabitants of the world will readily
receive the mark of the Beast (Antichrist) on either their foreheads
or hands. As we've learned, this mark is not just to allow people
to buy and sell food as well as live without persecution. No,
ultimately, it will be a sign indicating that they pledged allegiance
to Satan, having willfully rejected the God of heaven and spurned

the offer of salvation through Christ Jesus. The consequence is that they will now receive in their flesh punishment from God for their open rejection – with grotesque and painful sores. Their God-cursing and pervasive evil will be dealt with by God, both on earth through the seven plague judgments and for all eternity in the eternal lake of fire (hell).

* **Revelation 16:3-7** → The second and third angels pour out their bowls of God's judgment in response to the open and defiant murder of Christ's followers during the time of the Tribulation. Even today, news reports detail conflicts across the globe where people openly gloat over the killing of others. This will increase dramatically during the Great Tribulation. Those targeted for mass murder will be people who have chosen allegiance to God versus allegiance to Satan. Since the world's inhabitants will rejoice in spilling the blood of God's people, God in turn will give them blood to drink from the sea, rivers, springs and wells. As stated in verse seven, God's judgments are true and they are just. Galatians 6:7-9 reiterates this truth:

> Do not be deceived: God cannot be mocked. A man reaps what he sows. The one who sows to please his sinful nature, from that nature will reap destruction; the one who sows to please the Spirit, from the Spirit will reap eternal life. Let us not become weary in doing good, for at the proper time we will reap a harvest if we do not give up.

Scorching Heat and Agonizing Darkness

Revelation 16:8-11

[8] *The fourth angel poured out his bowl on the sun, and the sun was given power to scorch people*

209

*with fire. * ^{9} *They were seared by the intense heat and they cursed the name of God, who had control over these plagues, but they refused to repent and glorify him. * ^{10} *The fifth angel poured out his bowl on the throne of the beast, and his kingdom was plunged into darkness. Men gnawed their tongues in agony * ^{11} *and cursed the God of heaven because of their pains and their sores, but they refused to repent of what they had done.*

* Revelation 16:8-9 → Many people today, as well as those who will be living during the future scene described in these two verses, have a passion for nature and the environment. One major topic of interest today is global warming. While protecting the environment is an important area of focus for us all, sadly, many focus on slowing down arctic melts and reducing the damage of our ozone layer but deliberately remove God from their equation of living. During this fourth bowl judgment, God will cause a form of "global warming" the world has never seen. The depth of sin and depravity in the world during this judgment from God is summed in the attitudes of the world's inhabitants, who "...they cursed the name of God, who had control over these plagues, but they refused to repent and glorify him." [Revelation 16:9] Again, God's judgment and wrath, poured out on his creation which has rejected Him, are just and righteous.

* Revelation 16:10-11 → Yet another judgment of God that reveals why His acts are justified. In utter darkness, all activities of people in the Antichrist's kingdom will come to a screeching halt. With this darkness will come lootings, riots, and fear. But even while experiencing this fifth bowl judgment, the world's inhabitants who take the mark of the Beast (Antichrist) still refuse to repent and glorify the God of heaven.

Chapter 31

Demons, Earthquakes and Armageddon

Revelation 16:12-21

Apocalypse: "Now all shall bear witness to my greatness! I hold their leaders powerless and their mightiest city is under my control. Soon, I shall show this world a war the likes of which has never been seen! I will weed out the weak and inferior so that only the strong survive!"

[X-Men Legends II Rise of Apocalypse]

The words of Apocalypse are but a foreshadowing of the pompous statements that will be made by the future world leader referred to in the Bible as the Beast out the Abyss (the Antichrist). He will make great boasts, openly worship Satan, and demand to be worshiped by the world's inhabitants. Deceived and deceiving others, he will pit the world's armies against Jesus at his second coming. This foolish move will be his last, for Jesus will then demonstrate to the world why he is the colossal juggernaut of heaven – unstoppable, irresistible, and unlimited in power. It is Jesus who will do the weeding out of people. Jesus explained this to His disciples after teaching them a parable about weeds in Matthew 13:24-30:

> Then he left the crowd and went into the house. His
> disciples came to him and said, "Explain to us the

parable of the weeds in the field." He answered, "The one who sowed the good seed is the Son of Man. The field is the world, and the good seed stands for the people of the kingdom. The weeds are the people of the evil one, and the enemy who sows them is the devil. The harvest is the end of the age, and the harvesters are angels. "As the weeds are pulled up and burned in the fire, so it will be at the end of the age. The Son of Man will send out his angels, and they will weed out of his kingdom everything that causes sin and all who do evil. They will throw them into the blazing furnace, where there will be weeping and gnashing of teeth. Then the righteous will shine like the sun in the kingdom of their Father. Whoever has ears, let them hear. [Matthew 13:36-43]

A Waterless Euphrates River and Three Evil Spirits

Revelation 16:12-16

[12] *The sixth angel poured out his bowl on the great river Euphrates, and its water was dried up to prepare the way for the kings from the East.* [13] *Then I saw three evil spirits that looked like frogs; they came out of the mouth of the dragon, out of the mouth of the beast and out of the mouth of the false prophet.* [14] *They are spirits of demons performing miraculous signs, and they go out to the kings of the whole world, to gather them for the battle on the great day of God Almighty.* [15] *"Behold, I come like a thief! Blessed is he who stays*

awake and keeps his clothes with him, so that he may not go naked and be shamefully exposed." [16] *Then they gathered the kings together to the place that in Hebrew is called Armageddon.*

* **Revelation 16:12** → Armies from countries east of the Euphrates River will march against Israel to destroy it. Satan will demonically influence, lead, and control world leaders who are bent on Israel's destruction and the rejection of all things pertaining to God.

* **Revelation 16:13-14** → The three evil spirits that look like frogs will emerge from the insides of the Dragon (Satan), the beast that came out of the Abyss (Antichrist), and the beast that came out of the earth (False Prophet). These evil and deceptive spirits will possess world leaders and cause them to unite for war against Israel. As the world's armies converge on the Holy Land, Christ the King will make his grand entrance back into the world as the conquering and redeeming God.

* **Revelation 16:15-16** → The word Armageddon is only used one time in the Bible, found in Revelation 16:16. It does not actually refer to an event, but a place. "Armageddon" is the Greek rendering of the Hebrew word Megiddo. In the world of geography, Megiddo is defined not as a mountain, but as a "tell or tel": a type of archaeological mound created by human occupation and abandonment of a geographical site over many centuries."[11] It is at this location that the kings of the whole world will be gathered for battle, bringing with them their armies, air forces, and naval fleets.

The World's Greatest Earthquake and Boulder-Sized Hail

Revelation 16:17-21

> [17] *The seventh angel poured out his bowl into the air, and out of the temple came a loud voice from the throne, saying, "It is done!"* [18] *Then there came flashes of lightning, rumblings, peals of thunder and a severe earthquake. No earthquake like it has ever occurred since man has been on earth, so tremendous was the quake.* [19] *The great city split into three parts, and the cities of the nations collapsed. God remembered Babylon the Great and gave her the cup filled with the wine of the fury of his wrath.* [20] *Every island fled away and the mountains could not be found.* [21] *From the sky huge hailstones of about a hundred pounds each fell upon men. And they cursed God on account of the plague of hail, because the plague was so terrible.*

* **Revelation 16:17-20** → This global earthquake will make all others in the history of mankind look like a light tremor that goes unnoticed. There will be mass destruction of nations and unprecedented loss of lives. Mountains will collapse and islands will be completely buried under global tsunamis.

* **Revelation 16:21** → On July 23, 2010, a violent thunderstorm struck Vivian, South Dakota and produced hailstones that were softball-sized and larger. The largest hailstone ever recorded in the United States was found on that day, measuring "8.0 inches in diameter and weighed nearly 2 pounds (1 pound, 15 ounces) with a circumference of 18.62 inches."[12] To give you a frame of reference, a baseball's circumference is nine inches. So the size of the hailstones referenced in this verse

of the Apocalypse will be enormous – like large rocks and small boulders falling from the sky. These will be like miniature bombs going off – destroying property and killing many people and living things.

Chapter 32

The Mystery Woman: Intoxicating Danger

Revelation 17:1-5

MUTANT INSIGHT

Apocalypse: "Submit! Come, cleave unto me. And know the joy of eternal darkness."

[X-Men The Animated Series: Obsession]

O nce again, the writers of the X-Men Animated Series used the Bible as the basis for some of Apocalypse's powerful statements. The one above is adapted from Jesus' words to all who are worn out from trying to live without him regarding the love, joy, peace, hope, and contentment that he alone offers:

> Come to me, all you who are weary and burdened, and I will give you rest. Take my yoke upon you and learn from me, for I am gentle and humble in heart, and you will find rest for your souls. For my yoke is easy and my burden is light. [Matthew 11:28-30]

You've probably figured this out, but there is no joy in eternal darkness. Jesus says that eternal darkness has only regret, gnashing of teeth, and everlasting suffering. Submit? Yes! But only to God, through Jesus Christ.

The Woman on the Beast

Revelation 17:1-4

> [1] *One of the seven angels who had the seven bowls came and said to me, "Come, I will show you the punishment of the great prostitute, who sits on many waters.* [2] *With her the kings of the earth committed adultery and the inhabitants of the earth were intoxicated with the wine of her adulteries."* [3] *Then the angel carried me away in the Spirit into a desert. There I saw a woman sitting on a scarlet beast that was covered with blasphemous names and had seven heads and ten horns.* [4] *The woman was dressed in purple and scarlet, and was glittering with gold, precious stones and pearls. She held a golden cup in her hand, filled with abominable things and the filth of her adulteries.*

* **Revelation 17:1** → The prostitute referred to in these verses is the nefarious religious system of the Antichrist, headed by the False Prophet. The foundation and essence of this satanically-concocted religious system was birthed in the Garden of Eden. The information being relayed in Revelation 17 and 18 is of supreme importance. These two chapters reveal the root of Satan's deception used on Eve, Adam, and all of creation, right to the present day. The phrase "...who sits on many waters" simply refers to the prostitute's global presence and influence. It (the prostitute) rests upon a system of beliefs and worship created to deceive the nations and aims to corrupt both God's creation and his plan of redeeming mankind through Christ Jesus.

* **Revelation 17:2** → The adultery of the kings of the world with the prostitute, along with the "inhabitants of the earth who are intoxicated with the wine of her adulteries", speak to the global influence (past, present, and future) of the prostitute and the spiritual compromise (spiritual unfaithfulness) that she will cause the majority of the earth's population to commit against God Almighty.

* **Revelation 17:3** → In this verse the angel translates John from heaven to a desert to see the prostitute sitting on a scarlet beast (the seven-headed nations-beast that John saw come out of the sea). The Antichrist, the beast who comes up from the Abyss, is referred to in Revelation 17:11 as an eighth king who will emerge from the seventh king (the seventh head of the beast out of the sea). He will rule the confederation of ten nations and its world leaders. The phrase "sitting on a scarlet beast" implies that the religious system has its origin, base, power, and position resting on (or in) Satan.

* **Revelation 17:4** → The colors and adornment of the prostitute are significant. In the Bible, the color scarlet is often associated with priests, spiritual sacrifice and wealth [Exodus 38:18, Leviticus 14:4, Josh 2:8, II Samuel: 1:24, Isaiah 1:18, Matthew 27:28]. Purple was also used in the areas of spirituality and wealth [Judges 8:26, Daniel 5:7, Esther 8:15, Luke 16:19]. Likewise, gold and precious stones were also associated with the priesthood and royalty.

However, while the woman on the beast may have an appearance of religion/devotion to God, her colors and adornment are where the comparison to anything holy ends. Rather than being filled with the pure and glorious things of God, her cup is filled with the abominable and filthy adulteries to her everlasting shame and contempt. The filthy adulteries begin first and foremost with the want-to-be king of heaven, Satan. Beyond him, the prostitution (again, defined as spiritual adultery and compromise) is with nations, kings, and the one-world religion philosophy of the ages.

Sensual, Satanic, and Sentenced to Destruction

Revelation 17:5

⁵ *This title was written on her forehead: MYS-TERY, BABYLON THE GREAT, THE MOTHER OF PROSTITUES, AND OF THE ABOMINATIONS OF THE EARTH.*

* **Revelation 17:5** → This verse gives us more details as to who the prostitute is, based on the inscription we read that is on her forehead. Let's examine each of the words and phrases:

MYSTERY: As stated in the analysis of 17:1, the satanic religious system depicted as the prostitute began in the Garden of Eden with the deception that caused Adam and Eve's disobedience/rebellion. Sin and death were introduced into the world when Satan tempted Eve (and subsequently, Adam) to act in disobedience to God. Satan opposed the word/command of God, telling Eve that she wouldn't die (physically and spiritually) if she ate of the tree. On the contrary, he told her that she and Adam would actually become *like* God if they had the knowledge that could be gained by eating the fruit. Satan told her that the knowledge that God has, a mystery to she and Adam, could be theirs if they listened to him.

The Greek word for "knowledge" is *gnosis*. When Adam and Eve were deceived by Satan, Gnosticism was born. It is the Satan-inspired religion of secret knowledge that supposedly sets one free from the constraints of this earthly existence (by freeing one from the rules, boundaries, and restrictions of God to do/be whatever one wants). The foundation of just about every religious philosophy that is counter to biblical Christianity has its origin in Gnosticism.

BABYLON THE GREAT: In Genesis 10:6-12 the Bible speaks of Nimrod, one of Noah's great-grandsons. He was the first builder of cities, including making Babylon one of the first centers of his vast kingdom [Genesis 10:10]. Genesis 11:1-9 tells the story of the Tower of Babel and Nimrod's attempt to construct a one-world government and religious system, with Gnosticism as the root of their belief system. As stated in Genesis 11:4, Nimrod's goal was to have mankind ascend to the heavens on their own and have them be their own gods (be their own authority with no desire to obey and be accountable to God).

God did not endorse this rebellion and broke up Nimrod's plan by causing people to be scattered into various new languages (prior to that, all people on the earth spoke one language). Today, various world religions of the world have similarities because they have the same origin...Babylon. Later in history (605 BC), Babylon again became the world power under the rule of Nebuchadnezzar.

THE MOTHER OF PROSTITUTES (The Queen of Heaven) AND OF THE ABOMINATIONS OF THE EARTH: The religious system first established in Babylon by Nimrod has continued throughout history, carried to every tribe and nation after God thwarted man's plans for the Tower of Babel. Gnosticism has been disguised in various ways by Satan throughout the years. He always tries to copy (with deceit and deadly consequences) what God does, using wolves in sheep clothing to deceive the unsuspecting masses:

> For such people are false apostles, deceitful work-
> ers, masquerading as apostles of Christ. And no
> wonder, for Satan himself masquerades as an angel
> of light. It is not surprising, then, if his servants also
> masquerade as servants of righteousness. Their end
> will be what their actions deserve. [II Corinthians
> 11:13-15].

In Genesis 3:15 God addresses Satan after the deception of Adam and Eve:

> And I will put enmity between you and the woman, and between your seed and hers; he will crush your head, and you will strike his heel.

Tucked away in this one verse is the first prophecy of the virgin birth of the Messiah, Jesus Christ. When Satan received this condemnation from God, he began crafting his deceptive response and attack on the minds – and eternal destiny – of all he might deceive. The core of the gnostic-based, one world religion will be associated with what emerged from the Nimrod era, including a counterfeit teaching of the virgin birth associated with Nimrod's wife Sermiramis. After Nimrod's death, she publicly declared that he had been resurrected as the god of the sun. As the sun god, he supposedly used his sun rays to miraculously inseminate her with a child (Satan's counterfeit story of a virgin birth). The child's name was Tammuz, whom she claimed was the reincarnated Nimrod. Thus, Semiramis was both Nimrod's wife (queen of heaven) and mother. With the scattering of the world's population that occurred at the Tower of Babel, this false story of the miraculous conception and birth of the child spread throughout the world, forming the foundation for pagan religious practices. Some of the different names for Semiramis and her child, Tammuz, that arose across the world are:

- Phoenicia → Ashtoreth and Tammuz

- Egypt → Isis and Horus (Horus is symbolized by an all-seeing eye – even pictured on the U.S. Dollar.)

- Greece → Aphrodite and Eros

- Italy → Venus and Cupid

- Phrygia (Asia Turkey) → Cybele and Attis

God considers the Satan-inspired heresy of the queen of heaven and the false virgin birth to be a primary adversary to the truth of his purposes and plan for redeeming mankind. He addressed (and rebuked) Israel for its spiritual adultery in worshiping the Queen of Heaven (The Mother of Prostitutes religion). Consider these Bible passages illustrating this satanic practice:

> We will burn incense to the Queen of Heaven and will pour out drink offerings to her just as we and our ancestors, our kings and our officials did in the towns of Judah and in the streets of Jerusalem. At that time we had plenty of food and were well off and suffered no harm. But ever since we stopped burning incense to the Queen of Heaven and pouring out drink offerings to her, we have had nothing and have been perishing by sword and famine." The women added, "When we burned incense to the Queen of Heaven and poured out drink offerings to her, did not our husbands know that we were making cakes impressed with her image and pouring out drink offerings to her? [Jeremiah 44:17-19]

> In the sixth year, in the sixth month on the fifth day, while I was sitting in my house and the elders of Judah were sitting before me, the hand of the Sovereign Lord came on me there…He said to me, "Son of man, have you seen what the elders of Israel are doing in the darkness, each at the shrine of his own idol? They say, 'The Lord does not see us; the Lord has forsaken the land.'" Again, he said, "You will see them doing things that are even more detestable."

Then he brought me to the entrance of the north gate of the house of the Lord, and I saw women sitting there, mourning the god Tammuz. He said to me, "Do you see this, son of man? You will see things that are even more detestable than this." He then brought me into the inner court of the house of the Lord, and there at the entrance to the temple, between the portico and the altar, were about twenty-five men. With their backs toward the temple of the Lord and their faces toward the east, they were bowing down to the sun in the east. He said to me, "Have you seen this, son of man? Is it a trivial matter for the people of Judah to do the detestable things they are doing here? Must they also fill the land with violence and continually arouse my anger? Look at them putting the branch to their nose! Therefore I will deal with them in anger; I will not look on them with pity or spare them. Although they shout in my ears, I will not listen to them." [Ezekiel 8:1-18]

As stated earlier, this Satan-inspired religion can be found not only in the Old Testament of the Bible, but also in the New Testament. Acts 19:23-41 give details of the apostle Paul's encounter in the city of Ephesus with the worshippers of the Greek goddess Artemis (Roman goddess Diana), also referred to as "the Queen of Heaven":

About that time there arose a great disturbance about the Way. A silversmith named Demetrius, who made silver shrines of Artemis, brought in a lot of business for the craftsmen there. He called them together, along with the workers in related trades, and said: "You know, my friends, that we receive a good income from this business. And you see and hear how this fellow Paul has convinced and led astray large numbers of people here in Ephesus and in practically the whole province of Asia. He says that gods made by human hands are no gods at all. There is danger not only that our trade will lose its good name, but also that the temple of the great goddess Artemis will be discredited; and the goddess herself, who is worshiped throughout the province of Asia and the world, will be robbed of her divine majesty." When they heard this, they were furious and began shouting: "Great is Artemis of the Ephesians!" Soon the whole city was in an uproar. ..The city clerk quieted the crowd and said: "Fellow Ephesians, doesn't all the world know that the city of Ephesus is the guardian of the temple of the great Artemis and of her image, which fell from heaven? Therefore, since these facts are undeniable, you ought to calm down and not do anything rash... [Acts 19:23-41]

Wow, it's amazing what we can learn from the Bible if we really take the time to read it. By way of direct and indirect worship of the Mother of prostitutes ("Queen of Heaven"), multitudes throughout history in almost every nation have sought to live according to various mystical philosophies launched in Babylon, in search of the gnosis (hidden, or "secret" knowledge).

Chapter 33

The Prostitute on the Beast: Out for Blood

Revelation 17:6-14

Apocalypse: "And so it shall come to pass that all existence will end – except that which is here within the axis (of time) outside of time. Then shall I begin anew, recreating the universe in my own image; a perfect universe where I shall rule unchallenged!"
Magneto: "When you sought my help, you said nothing of this madness…"
Apocalypse: "Then you were fool enough to believe me. Strike him down my horsemen!"

[X-Men The Animated Series: Beyond Good and Evil Part 4]

The exchange above between Apocalypse and Magneto prove that it is foolish to trust others who are evil and demented. Magneto knew that something was not quite right with Apocalypse's character and plans. Magneto's moral compass, while a bit stained over the years, will not allow him to go along with the eradication of all life – including weaker mutants – so that Apocalypse could accomplish his goals.

The good news of the apocalypse (revelation) of God through Jesus Christ is that the fate of world will not involve the ending of all things in existence. While he will do away with Satan and all who worship him, God promises eternal life to all who come to him for forgiveness of sins and the promise of eternal life.

Mystery of the Woman and Beast

Revelation 17:6-8

⁶ I saw that the woman was drunk with the blood of the saints, the blood of those who bore testimony to Jesus. When I saw her, I was greatly astonished. ⁷ Then the angel said to me: "Why are you astonished? I will explain to you the mystery of the woman and of the beast she rides, which has the seven heads and ten horns. ⁸ The beast, which you saw, once was, now is not, and will come up out of the Abyss and go to his destruction. The inhabitants of the earth whose names have not been written in the book of life from the creation of the world will be astonished when they see the beast, because he once was, now is not, and yet will come.

* **Revelation 17:6-7** → John sees the Prostitute and is astonished. Why? Because of its vast influence, size, power, splendor, and deceptive masquerade that has led multitudes on the earth into idolatry. John is given a panoramic view of the woman's influence on the earth through the annals of time – from the time after the great flood (Noah) until prior to the second coming of Jesus.

* **Revelation 17:8** → The words, "The beast, which you saw" refer to the vision that John saw of Antichrist ruling during the future time of the Tribulation. The words, "once was" refer to the Antichrist's rule in the past, prior to the revelation being given to him. The words "now is not", refer to the fact that at the time of the revelation being given to John (about 90 A.D., 60 years after

Jesus' crucifixion, resurrection, and ascension into heaven), the beast was not alive – but had been previously. The words "and will come up out of the Abyss and go to his destruction" mean that this is a former renowned world-leader who has been kept alive in the Abyss but will be allowed to be released, come back to live on earth, and rule the federation of ten nations during the Great Tribulation. When this person died in the past, God sent him to the Abyss, to be held for release in the future time of the Tribulation. The Abyss is a horrid place where God has bound various evil spirits and creatures. Evil spirits are terrified of the Abyss, as evidenced in an encounter that some of them had with Jesus during his earthly ministry (see Luke 8:29-33, which we examined in our discussion of Revelation 9:2). Upon being released from the Abyss, the world will see him alive again (healed from a previous fatal wound) and be astonished (refer back to Revelation 13:3).

Seven Heads, Seven Hills, Seven Kings

Revelation 17:9-14

[9] *"This calls for a mind with wisdom. The seven heads are seven hills on which the woman sits.* [10] *They are also seven kings. Five have fallen, one is, the other has not yet come; but when he does come, he must remain for a little while.* [11] *The beast who once was, and now is not, is an eighth king. He belongs to the seven and is going to his destruction.* [12] *"The ten horns you saw are ten kings who have not yet received a kingdom, but who for one hour will receive authority as kings along with the beast.* [13] *They have one purpose and will give their power and authority to the*

beast. [14] They will make war against the Lamb, but the Lamb will overcome them because he is Lord of lords and King of kings—and with him will be his called, chosen and faithful followers."

* Revelation 17:9-14 → The Antichrist will rise to power as the Satan-led man who will aim to bring further corruption to God's purpose for mankind (which is to worship God and keep his commands). The Antichrist will join the seven-country federation and become its leader. Eventually, he will add ten more kings to his unholy federation and foolishly declare war on the returning Lamb of God (Jesus). Regarding the success of Antichrist's satanically empowered attempt to fight against Jesus, in conjunction with verse fourteen:

> And then the lawless one [Antichrist] will be revealed, whom the Lord Jesus will overthrow with the breath of his mouth and destroy by the splendor of his coming. [II Thessalonians 2:8]

Betrayed and Devoured

Revelation 17:15-18

[15] Then the angel said to me, "The waters you saw, where the prostitute sits, are peoples, multitudes, nations and languages. [16] The beast and the ten horns you saw will hate the prostitute. They will bring her to ruin and leave her naked; they will eat her flesh and burn her with fire. [17] For God has put it into their hearts to accomplish his purpose by agreeing to give the beast their power to rule, until God's words are fulfilled. [18] The woman you

saw is the great city that rules over the kings of the earth."

* **Revelation 17:15-18** → The Antichrist, with his federation of ten kings and their nations, will destroy the prostitute. Satan will have no need for the prostitute anymore because he will want direct control and worship centered on him – not desiring to share any of his "glory" with the prostitute (Queen of Heaven) – the dominant and global religious system. Also, keep in mind what God says in Galatians 6:7: "Do not be deceived, God is not mocked; for whatever a man sows, that he will also reap." The prostitute will sow deception, greed, adultery, lust, murder and will be betrayed and destroyed.

Chapter 34

The Mystery Woman: Fallen and Ruined

Revelation 18:1-24

Apocalypse: "Beast, how many peoples have dreamed of my end? You are no closer than the Babylonians with their swords and fire-sticks!"

[X-Men The Animated Series: Obsession]

I n preparation for the battle of Armageddon, as reviewed in Revelation 16, evil spirits from Satan, the Antichrist, and the False Prophet will go across the globe and possess the kings and leaders of the world. Their purpose will be to direct these leaders to fight against the Holy One, Jesus, who will descend from heaven in majestic glory, power, and honor. For all who hate him and want to be his adversary, all I have to say is what Mr. T. used to say back in the day: "I pity the fool!"

The Fall of Babylon

Revelation 18:1-4

¹ *After this I saw another angel coming down from heaven. He had great authority, and the*

earth was illuminated by his splendor. ² *With a mighty voice he shouted: "Fallen! Fallen is Babylon the Great! She has become a home for demons and a haunt for every evil spirit, a haunt for every unclean and detestable bird.* ³ *For all the nations have drunk the maddening wine of her adulteries. The kings of the earth committed adultery with her, and the merchants of the earth grew rich from her excessive luxuries."* ⁴ *Then I heard another voice from heaven say: "Come out of her, my people, so that you will not share in her sins, so that you will not receive any of her plagues;*

* **Revelation 18:1** → John sees another angel with great power and splendor descend from heaven. As we have learned thus far in our journey through the book of the Revelation of Jesus Christ, there are mighty beings in God's universe whom the inhabitants of this world will one day encounter in ways never before experienced. My hope is that people will be in awe of neither them nor their power but, instead, be in awe of the great God of the universe who created these beings, bowing down to him in reverence, submission, and obedience.

* **Revelation 18:2-3** → The majority of people in the world today don't consider demonic activity (or unclean spirits) relevant or even real. They watch television shows, movies, and video games that glamorize and even glorify Satan, demons, vampires, ghosts, and zombies. They laugh, cheer, and exclaim how much they "love" the macabre genre. That is sad! To love that which is evil, grim and ghastly is not honoring to God. He is about love and life. Satan is about darkness and death. In these verses, the angel tells John that evil will characterize the future Babylon the Great, in which Satan will have his seat of authority, ruling and influencing the world. We've all heard the word "haunted" used in various contexts. The word haunt means,

"a place frequented by a specified person or group". Verse two indicates that Babylon the Great will be a haunt for every evil spirit. Demonic possession, oppression, and utter evil will run rampant.

* **Revelation 18:4** → John hears another voice call out to a group of whom God refers to as "my people". Who are they? They are those who refused to take the mark of the beast (Antichrist) and who have placed their faith in the Lord Jesus Christ. These are people who will choose to be in allegiance with the Lord, shun evil, and will be his courageous ambassadors in the world. Sadly, many of the pastors and biblical teachers today rarely touch the subject of how Satan is still using demonic influence (oppression, depression and even possession) to keep people captive to various forms of mental deception, spiritual bondage, and lives of depravity as described in Galatians 5:19-21:

> The acts of the flesh are obvious: sexual immorality, impurity and debauchery; idolatry and witchcraft; hatred, discord, jealousy, fits of rage, selfish ambi-tion, dissensions, factions and envy; drunkenness, orgies, and the like. I warn you, as I did before, that those who live like this will not inherit the kingdom of God.

Yet, the first four books of the New Testament show Jesus consistently warning his followers to be on guard against Satan and demonic influences. Very often he diagnosed people's deep issues as being neither mental illnesses nor problems needing medicinal solutions. On the contrary, he categorized a range of physical disabilities, mental issues, and internal diseases as being demonically-related. He frequently cast out evil spirits that were possessing and/or oppressing such people.

Why did Jesus refer to demons and hell more than he did heaven during his earthly ministry (first four books of the New

Testament)? Because he was (and still is) stating clearly that if we believe him and his word, we should take Satan's influence in the world very seriously. Satan is not referred to in the Bible as the "god of this world" [II Corinthians 4] for merely random and trivial reasons. No, revisiting what God says about the spiritual realm is critical. We must heed His warnings, obey His commands, and strive to grow in the grace, knowledge and power of Christ Jesus to combat the deceptive strategies of Satan.

Many reading this may have family members and friends who are shackled in one or more ways by the evil one. We may be the only person in their sphere of relationships who can point them to the only One who can set them free: King Jesus, the Great Physician. Will you humbly seek God in prayer and then boldly, in the power of the Lord, go to those you love with persistence, passion, and purpose – allowing Jesus, by His Spirit, to work in and through you to heal and free those you care about? If not, here is the sobering question: Do you really love and care for them?

The Prostitute's Detailed Downfall

Revelation 18:5-19

> [5] *for her sins are piled up to heaven, and God has remembered her crimes.* [6] *Give back to her as she has given; pay her back double for what she has done. Mix her a double portion from her own cup.* [7] *Give her as much torture and grief as the glory and luxury she gave herself. In her heart she boasts, 'I sit as queen; I am not a widow, and I will never mourn.'* [8] *Therefore in one day her plagues will overtake her: death, mourning and famine. She will be consumed by fire, for mighty is the*

Lord God who judges her. [9] *"When the kings of the earth who committed adultery with her and shared her luxury see the smoke of her burning, they will weep and mourn over her.* [10] *Terrified at her torment, they will stand far off and cry: "'Woe! Woe, O great city, O Babylon, city of power! In one hour your doom has come!'* [11] *"The merchants of the earth will weep and mourn over her because no one buys their cargoes any more—* [12] *cargoes of gold, silver, precious stones and pearls; fine linen, purple, silk and scarlet cloth; every sort of citron wood, and articles of every kind made of ivory, costly wood, bronze, iron and marble;* [13] *cargoes of cinnamon and spice, of incense, myrrh and frankincense, of wine and olive oil, of fine flour and wheat; cattle and sheep; horses and carriages; and bodies and souls of men.* [14] *"They will say, 'The fruit you longed for is gone from you. All your riches and splendor have vanished, never to be recovered.'* [15] *The merchants who sold these things and gained their wealth from her will stand far off, terrified at her torment. They will weep and mourn* [16] *and cry out: "'Woe! Woe, O great city, dressed in fine linen, purple and scarlet, and glittering with gold, precious stones and pearls!* [17] *In one hour such great wealth has been brought to ruin!' "Every sea captain, and all who travel by ship, the sailors, and all who earn their living from the sea, will stand far off.* [18] *When they see the smoke of her burning, they will exclaim, 'Was there ever a city like this great city?'* [19] *They will throw dust on their heads, and with weeping and mourning cry out: "'Woe! Woe, O great city, where all who had ships on the sea became rich*

*through her wealth! In one hour she has been
brought to ruin!*

* **Revelation 18:5-19** → As a reminder, the context for
Revelation 18 began back in Revelation 16 with the seven angels
pouring out the seven bowl judgments of God. The time line
for those verses picks up from Revelation 16:17-21, when the
seventh angel poured out his judgment and there was a severe and
unprecedented global earthquake. The Bible says that the quake
will be so tremendous that Babylon the Great will be split into
three parts. Huge hailstones weighing about 100 pounds will fall
from the sky, crushing people and other things. Those affected
will continue to curse God rather than repent. In the span of
one hour, the base of Satan's worldwide system (governmental,
economic, religious) will topple. Jesus will be on his way to
reclaim his creation. His judgment is swift, just, and unstoppable.

Weeping Sailors and A Powerful Angel

Revelation 18:20-24

*[20] Rejoice over her, O heaven! Rejoice, saints and
apostles and prophets! God has judged her for
the way she treated you."' [21] Then a mighty angel
picked up a boulder the size of a large millstone
and threw it into the sea, and said: "With such
violence the great city of Babylon will be thrown
down, never to be found again. [22] The music of
harpists and musicians, flute players and trum-
peters, will never be heard in you again. No work-
man of any trade will ever be found in you again.
The sound of a millstone will never be heard in
you again. [23] The light of a lamp will never shine
in you again. The voice of bridegroom and bride*

will never be heard in you again. Your merchants were the world's great men. By your magic spell all the nations were led astray. [24] *In her was found the blood of prophets and of the saints, and of all who have been killed on the earth."*

* **Revelation 18:20** → God will judge the satanically-governed Babylon the Great—the economic, political, and religious system that has been intertwined in the world—for its persecution of prophets (during the Old Testament period), apostles (during the period shortly after Christ's resurrection), and God's holy people (during the time from Christ's resurrection through the time of the declaration of verse twenty).

* **Revelation 18:21** → This verse does not give us the dimensions of the large millstone referenced. To give you a feel of the size and weight of large millstones, consider this: one that is six feet in diameter and two-and-a-half feet thick would weigh approximately 10,600 pounds. So, whether the boulder was smaller or lager, one thing we know for sure is that this angel is one strong being!

* **Revelation 18:22-24** → Revelation 18:22-23 reveal that everyday life will be continuing in Babylon the Great just before God's final judgment. Music will be performed, business will be conducted, and people will be marrying – all while living in a society devoid of godliness and that rejoices when the righteous are killed.

Chapter 35

The Wedding Banquet of the Lamb

Revelation 19:1-10

MUTANT INSIGHT

Sunfire: "Apocalypse has priests?"
Emma Frost: "Oh yes. True to his egomaniacal form, Apocalypse has built an entire cult that worships him."

[X-Men, Legends II: Rise of Apocalypse]

S hintoism, the Japanese religious belief of Sunfire, teaches that Japan is the country of the gods and that Japanese people are the descendants of the gods. Thus, he is startled to find that Apocalypse claims to be divine and even has others (humans and mutants) worshiping him. Emma Frost brings clarity to Sunfire's confusion. Apocalypse, like all other pride-filled people, is suffering from an over-inflated view of himself. Her statement about his cult following is all-important considering God's warning about bowing down to false gods and idols. God alone is to be worshiped.

Most people have heard of the Ten Commandments, which God gave to the Hebrew people when they came out of their years of slavery in Egypt. The first three of these commands are found in Exodus 20:3-7:

> You shall have no other gods before me. You shall
> not make for yourself an image in the form of any-

thing in heaven above or on the earth beneath or in the waters below. You shall not bow down to them or worship them; for I, the Lord your God, am a jealous God, punishing the children for the sin of the parents to the third and fourth generation of those who hate me, but showing love to a thousand generations of those who love me and keep my commandments. You shall not misuse the name of the Lord your God, for the Lord will not hold anyone guiltless who misuses his name.

The word "worship" is defined as "the act of showing excessive admiration, respect, and love for someone or something." Since you have taken the time to read this book, it is my hope that you will take the next step and seriously examine your heart's devotions and investment of time, talent, and treasure to determine who (or what) you are worshiping. It has been said that you can easily tell what a person treasures and adores. Just examine where they spend their money and their time. Jesus says the following in Matthew 6:21 and 24:

> For where your treasure is, there your heart will be also...No one can serve two masters. Either you will hate the one and love the other, or you will be devoted to the one and despise the other. You cannot serve both God and money.

The remarkably successful music group U2 had a 1987 hit song entitled, "I Still Haven't Found What I'm Looking For". The lyrics of the song describe the cry of a person struggling with a divided heart of worship. While this person believes in the Lord and desires to walk with Him, he finds himself still empty, wandering in a "middle-land" of indecision, committing neither fully to sin (idols) nor to the Lord. Today, connect Matthew 6:24

with Proverbs 2:1-5 and walk with complete resolution to follow the Lord.

Thunderous Praise to God

Revelation 19:1-6

> [1] *After this I heard what sounded like the roar of a great multitude in heaven shouting: "Hallelujah! Salvation and glory and power belong to our God,* [2] *for true and just are his judgments. He has condemned the great prostitute who corrupted the earth by her adulteries.*
>
> *He has avenged on her the blood of his servants."* [3] *And again they shouted: "Hallelujah! The smoke from her goes up for ever and ever."* [4] *The twenty-four elders and the four living creatures fell down and worshiped God, who was seated on the throne. And they cried: "Amen, Hallelujah!"* [5] *Then a voice came from the throne, saying: "Praise our God, all you his servants, you who fear him, both small and great!"* [6] *Then I heard what sounded like a great multitude, like the roar of rushing waters and like loud peals of thunder, shouting: "Hallelujah! For our Lord God Almighty reigns.*

* **Revelation 19:1-6** → John's attention is now turned back to heaven, where he hears the thunderous shouts of those in heaven. In these verses, the word "hallelujah" is shouted four times. Have you ever said (or heard) the word, hallelujah? Do you know what it means? It is a word derived from the Hebrew language which means, "praise the Lord".

Another fact: The word hallelujah is found only four times in the entire New Testament, and all four of those are in the first six verses of this chapter. So, while many people say, "hallelujah" quite often, the large percentage of them (sadly) have never read, studied, or been taught about this chapter of the Bible and its eternal ramifications. Strive to know what God is imploring us to learn: his future plans and how we should wisely align ourselves with him and his sovereign rule. Life is *not* about personal glory. No, it is about the glory, honor, and praise of Almighty God. Revelation 19 is the end of the seven-year Tribulation period, with the last and defining act being the glorious second return of the Lord Jesus Christ to earth.

A Heavenly Wedding and Celebration

Revelation 19:7-10

> [7] *Let us rejoice and be glad and give him glory! For the wedding of the Lamb has come, and his bride has made herself ready.* [8] *Fine linen, bright and clean, was given her to wear." (Fine linen stands for the righteous acts of the saints.)* [9] *Then the angel said to me, "Write: 'Blessed are those who are invited to the wedding supper of the Lamb!'" And he added, "These are the true words of God."* [10] *At this I fell at his feet to worship him. But he said to me, "Do not do it! I am a fellow servant with you and with your brothers who hold to the testimony of Jesus. Worship God! For the testimony of Jesus is the spirit of prophecy."*

* **Revelation 19:7-10** → When I began writing this book, one of the hottest songs on Billboard's Top 100 was a rap song entitled, "Blessed", performed by multiple artists. Based on its lyrics and music video, the rappers state that God is blessing them, as proven by their material wealth, chosen lifestyles, and fame. One of them even says, "I cannot see heaven bein' much better than this…"

Such thinking, however, is flawed. Let me explain. The Bible makes it clear that even the vilest of persons can still benefit from the goodness of God's creation and natural laws. For example, whether a man is good or evil, he can receive the natural blessings of the sun on a beautiful spring day, the fresh air and picturesque views of walking through a beautiful forest, or relaxing on a tropical beach and watching the waves gently roll onto the sand.

Likewise, whether a man is good or evil, he can benefit from using his God-given talents to experience success in various ventures in life, such as sports, business, entertainment, and/ or investments. By using intellect, skills, and the assistance of associates, this person may be blessed by achieving great things. However, no such blessings experienced by living on earth (nature, money, fame) equate to the true blessings experienced in God's eternal economy. So who does God count "blessed" as pertaining to the true and eternal riches of his eternal kingdom? Jesus tells us clearly in one of his most famous sermons [Matthew 5:1-2]:

> Now when Jesus saw the crowds, he went up on a mountainside and sat down. His disciples came to him, and he began to teach them. He said: "*Blessed* are the poor in spirit, for theirs is the kingdom of heaven. *Blessed* are those who mourn, for they will be comforted. *Blessed* are the meek, for they will inherit the earth. *Blessed* are those who hunger and thirst for righteousness, for they will be filled. *Bless-*

ed are the merciful, for they will be shown mercy. *Blessed* are the pure in heart, for they will see God. *Blessed* are the peacemakers, for they will be called children of God. *Blessed* are those who are perse-cuted because of righteousness, for theirs is the kingdom of heaven. *Blessed* are you when people insult you, persecute you and falsely say all kinds of evil against you because of me. Rejoice and be glad, because great is your reward in heaven, for in the same way they persecuted the prophets who were before you." [Matthew 5:1-12, emphasis added]

Just think about this: Most three-year-old children feel blessed if they are given cheap plastic toys as gifts. However, those same people at sixteen years of age would not feel blessed at all if given those same toys. Similarly, grown men feel blessed when they acquire the "toys" of this world – such as exotic cars, luxurious yachts, and exquisite mansions. But when those same men step into eternity, whether in heaven or hell, they will look back on this temporal life's blessings just as a teen looks back at pre-school toys. Revelation 19:9 states that the truly blessed are those who are invited to the wedding supper of the Lamb. That blessing from the best gift-giver will continue for all eternity. So who are invited? Everyone. Will everyone be in attendance? No. Why not? Read the following story told by Jesus himself:

Jesus spoke to them again in parables, saying: 'The kingdom of heaven is like a king who prepared a wedding banquet for his son. He sent his servants to those who had been invited to the banquet to tell them to come, but they refused to come. Then he sent some more servants and said, "Tell those who have been invited that I have prepared my dinner: My oxen and fattened cattle have been butchered,

246

and everything is ready. Come to the wedding banquet." But they paid no attention and went off—one to his field, another to his business. The rest seized his servants, mistreated them and killed them. The king was enraged. He sent his army and destroyed those murderers and burned their city. Then he said to his servants, "The wedding banquet is ready, but those I invited did not deserve to come. So go to the street corners and invite to the banquet anyone you find." So the servants went out into the streets and gathered all the people they could find, the bad as well as the good, and the wedding hall was filled with guests. But when the king came in to see the guests, he noticed a man there who was not wearing wedding clothes. He asked, "How did you get in here without wedding clothes, friend?" The man was speechless. Then the king told the attendants, "Tie him hand and foot, and throw him outside, into the darkness, where there will be weeping and gnashing of teeth." For many are invited, but few are chosen. [Matthew 22:1-14]

The parable above, as well as other sections of Scripture, make clear that those invited to the wedding banquet of the Lamb, as seen in Revelation 19:9, are only those who belong to the body of Christ – the collective group of people who have trusted in Christ Jesus as their Savior and Lord, (also known as the church). In this chapter, the bride of the Lamb, another moniker given to the church, is made ready for the marriage supper of the Lamb. The church is "married" to Christ, meaning joined in eternal union [read Ephesians 5:22-33]. When the Wedding Supper of the Lamb is complete, Christ and his church, along with the angels, will prepare for their entry from heaven to earth (Jesus' second coming).

Chapter 36

The Conquering Rider on the White Horse

Revelation 19:11-21

Apocalypse: "Your powers are useless against me....Annoying insects; nothing can stop the Apocalypse. I cannot be harmed. Watch me and tremble as I bring the purity of oblivion to your world."

[X-Men The Animated Series: Time Fugitives, Part 1]

Proverbs 6:16-19 tells us the following:

> There are six things the Lord hates, seven that are detestable to him: haughty eyes, a lying tongue, hands that shed innocent blood, a heart that devises wicked schemes, feet that are quick to rush into evil, a false witness who pours out lies and a person who stirs up conflict in the community.

Clearly, Apocalypse's desires, motives, words, and actions would be detestable to God based on the preceding Bible verses. Note that the first detestable characteristic is haughty eyes, referring to a prideful attitude/posture. Apocalypse is fictitious, of course. But as we have read, there will be a large percentage of the earth's population alive at the second coming of Christ who will be deemed detestable. Certainly, Satan and the two beasts

249

(Antichrist and his False Prophet) are part of this anti-God group. Their punishment will be eternal, horrific, and justified.

The Rider on the White Horse

Revelation 19:11-18

> [11] *I saw heaven standing open and there before me was a white horse, whose rider is called Faithful and True. With justice he judges and makes war.* [12] *His eyes are like blazing fire, and on his head are many crowns. He has a name written on him that no one knows but he himself.* [13] *He is dressed in a robe dipped in blood, and his name is the Word of God.* [14] *The armies of heaven were following him, riding on white horses and dressed in fine linen, white and clean.* [15] *Out of his mouth comes a sharp sword with which to strike down the nations. "He will rule them with an iron scepter." He treads the winepress of the fury of the wrath of God Almighty.* [16] *On his robe and on his thigh he has this name written: King of kings and LORD of lords.* [17] *And I saw an angel standing in the sun, who cried in a loud voice to all the birds flying in midair, "Come, gather together for the great supper of God,* [18] *so that you may eat the flesh of kings, generals, and mighty men, of horses and their riders, and the flesh of all people, free and slave, small and great."*

* Revelation 19:11 → Jesus is the Faithful and True One. Note what he does in accordance with justice: He judges and makes war. Yes, this is Jesus. Don't buy into Satan's lies that portray Jesus as soft, or as one who overlooks and excuses sin and is not judgmental. In Matthew 10:34, during his first visit to earth, Jesus declared,

> Do not suppose that I have come to bring peace to the earth. I did not come to bring peace, but a sword.

Jesus is not to the one with whom one should trifle. He means business. The price He paid to atone for the world's sin, both in His horrific physical death and the unimaginable anguish of having the wrath of God the Father laid upon Him, because of our sin, is something that all people must deeply contemplate. We must then make the decision to either accept or reject Jesus' offer of a free pardon from the penalty of sin. Jesus came into the world for *one and only one* reason: to lay down His life as a ransom for the sins of the world. Whoever rejects Him is neither wise nor has a future of eternal life with God. Jesus will be only one of two things for each person at the end of their lives on earth: Faithful to save us or Faithful to condemn. The choice is ours. His second coming is to reclaim, rule, and rein on the earth, His creation.

> Then the Lord will go out and fight against those nations, as he fights on a day of battle. On that day his feet will stand on the Mount of Olives, east of Jerusalem, and the Mount of Olives will be split in two from east to west, forming a great valley, with half of the mountain moving north and half moving south. [Zechariah 14:3-4]

> For as lightning that comes from the east is visible even in the west, so will be the coming of the Son of Man. Wherever there is a carcass, there the vultures

will gather. Immediately after the distress of those days "the sun will be darkened, and the moon will not give its light; the stars will fall from the sky, and the heavenly bodies will be shaken." Then will appear the sign of the Son of Man in heaven. And then all the peoples of the earth will mourn when they see the Son of Man coming on the clouds of heaven, with power and great glory. [Matthew 24:27-30]

* **Revelation 19:12** → The reference to the Lord Jesus' eyes being like fire means that He knows and sees all things, even the secret things (one's motives, thoughts, words, actions) and will judge all things with his righteousness as the standard.

For the word of God is alive and active. Sharper than any double-edged sword, it penetrates even to dividing soul and spirit, joints and marrow; it judges the thoughts and attitudes of the heart. [13] Nothing in all creation is hidden from God's sight. Everything is uncovered and laid bare before the eyes of him to whom we must give account. [Hebrews 4:12-13.]

* **Revelation 19:13** → Jesus' robe will appear to have been dipped or bathed in blood because of what is about to occur in Revelation 19:14, which is His second coming to earth to wage war against the wicked inhabitants of the world. This will occur at the end of the Great Tribulation when the nations will be following Satan and the Antichrist. The Antichrist, along with his False Prophet, the kings of the earth, and their armies will gather in Israel with the initial goal of destroying Israel and Christians who have not yet been martyred. But when King Jesus is revealed at his second coming, these forces will foolishly unite to fight against Him.

Satan and his demonic forces will deceive the masses of people still living, convincing them that they can defeat the Lamb and finally liberate themselves from the restricting rules and presence of the Lord. They will they gather together for the final conflict – the Battle of Armageddon. For a graphic picture of Jesus on earth waging war during this time, check out the prophet Isaiah's vision and dialogue with Jesus concerning this day of vengeance and redemption – when He returns.

> "Who is this coming from Edom, from Bozrah, with his garments stained crimson? Who is this, robed in splendor, striding forward in the greatness of his strength? 'It is I, speaking in righteousness, mighty to save.' Why are your garments red, like those of one treading the winepress? 'I have trodden the winepress alone; from the nations no one was with me. I trampled them in my anger and trod them down in my wrath; their blood spattered my garments, and I stained all my clothing. For the day of vengeance was in my heart, and the year of my redemption has come. I looked, but there was no one to help, I was appalled that no one gave support; so my own arm worked salvation for me, and my own wrath sustained me. I trampled the nations in my anger; in my wrath I made them drunk and poured their blood on the ground.'" [Isaiah 63:1-6]

The reference in Revelation 19:13 to the name of Jesus being the Word of God is consistent with the message throughout all of the holy Scriptures: Jesus is God incarnate:

> In the beginning was the Word, and the Word was with God, and the Word was God. He was with God in the beginning. Through him all things were

made; without him nothing was made that has been made…He was in the world, and though the world was made through him, the world did not recognize him….The Word became flesh and made his dwelling among us. We have seen his glory, the glory of the one and only Son, who came from the Father, full of grace and truth. [John 1:1-3,10,14].

MUTANT INSIGHT

Apocalypse: "You can fire arrows from the tower of Babel, but you can never strike God!"

[X-Men: Apocalypse]

Apocalypse made the bold and blasphemous statement above to the X-Men after having captured Professor X and taken over Cerebro, the device that Professor X uses to amplify his renowned telepathic ability. Suffice it to say that his ego-driven claims of being God were silenced by those on the side of rightness and truth – proving that he was not God.

On the contrary, Jesus' claims of being God incarnate, both all-powerful and all-knowing, were validated by His birth, life, and resurrection. The armies of the world, at a future date during Armageddon, will learn full well why super-powered demons tremble in his presence. They will attempt to strike him but be decimated with finality.

---

* Revelation 19:14-16 → The armies of heaven refer to all people who during their lifetime on earth have acknowledged their sin before God, repented, and received Christ Jesus as Lord and Savior. This collective group of people is referred to as the church, which is the entire assembly of Jesus' followers. They will not engage in the battle of Armageddon. Jesus alone will deal with the rebellious humans on earth at the end of the Great Tribulation. Note that the apparel of this army is described as being "fine linen, white and clean".

* **Revelation 19:17-18** → Millions of people will comprise the armies of the world that will gather at Armageddon to fight against the Lamb. As Revelation 14:20 and 16:16 declare, the enemies of Jesus will be slain by Him in the wide plains of the Jezreel Valley, a region in which Armageddon is centered.

> During the past 4000 years, at least 34 bloody conflicts have already been fought at the ancient site of Megiddo and adjacent areas of the Jezreel Valley. Egyptians, Canaanites, Israelites, Midianites, Amalekites, Philistines, Hasmonaeans, Greeks, Romans, Muslims, Crusaders, Mamlukes, Mongols, French, Ottomans, British, Australians, Germans, Arabs and Israelis have all fought and died here. The names of the warring generals and leaders reverberate throughout history: Thutmose III, Deborah and Barak, Sisera, Gideon, Saul and Jonathan, Shishak, Jehu, Joram, Jezebel, Josiah, Antiochus, Ptolemy, Vespasian, Saladin, Napoleon, and Allenby, to name but a few of the most famous…Throughout history Megiddo and the Jezreel Valley have been Ground Zero for battles that determined the very course of civilization…There were so many battles in this little valley, which measures only 20 miles long by seven miles wide, that one might paraphrase Sir Winston Churchill and say "never in the field of hu-

man conflict have so many fought so often over so little space!"[13]

During the final battle, the blood of millions will flow from one end of this long valley to the other, rising as high as the horses' bridle. There will be blood everywhere. Yes, this is Jesus. He is loving, merciful, gracious, peaceful, and long-suffering. He is also holy and just. He offers everyone the chance to be pardoned of their sin and be forgiven. The goal of this book is to share the entire message of the Bible and make known to millions today the marvel of God's apocalypse. He loves you. Repent and trust Jesus today as your Savior and Lord. And let us not forget why the people have chosen to fight against Jesus. Re-read Revelation 16:12-16. Their destruction will be fully warranted!

The Battle of Armageddon

Revelation 19:19-21

> [19] *Then I saw the beast and the kings of the earth and their armies gathered together to make war against the rider on the horse and his army.* [20] *But the beast was captured, and with him the false prophet who had performed the miraculous signs on his behalf. With these signs he had deluded those who had received the mark of the beast and worshiped his image. The two of them were thrown alive into the fiery lake of burning sulfur.* [21] *The rest of them were killed with the sword that came out of the mouth of the rider on the horse, and all the birds gorged themselves on their flesh.*

* Revelation 19:19-20 → When Jesus comes back to make war against the nations and reclaim the earth, He will cast the Antichrist (the beast that came up from the Abyss) and his False Prophet (the second Beast, who came up from the earth) into hell (Gehenna). This is the eternal lake of fire where all who reject Christ will eternally be condemned. They will be the first two humans to be cast there. All other humans who have rejected God will be sent there as well after their own judgment [this will be discussed in the review of Revelation 20:11-15]. No one is currently in Gehenna. Since the rebellion in the garden of Eden, the souls of all deceased humans who rejected God's salvation go to a place also referred to in the Bible as Hades (also expressed in English as hell but is a place different than Gehenna). All in Hades, after their judgment (Romans 20:11-15), will be cast into Gehenna for eternal condemnation.

* Revelation 19:21 → Note that it is Jesus who does the fighting and killing of the world's armies that follow the Antichrist to battle Him. Then all of the birds called by the angel in verse seventeen gorge themselves on their flesh. Graphic? Yes! Serious? Yes! Have you trusted Jesus as Savior, Lord, and Friend?

Chapter 37

Utopia...Almost

Revelation 20:1-10

Apocalypse: "You presumed to attempt to destroy me mutant (Cable)? You shall pay for your hubris – right now!"

[X-Men The Animated Series:
Beyond Good and Evil (Part 1): The End of Time]

The word hubris means excessive pride, arrogance, or ego. Based on our reading of Revelation, it is clear that no one will stand before the Lord God Almighty with any bravado, cockiness, or pomp. All of His adversaries will be dealt with swiftly and eternally. Be sure that you decide wisely how you want to be addressed by Him: saint or sinner. Place your trust in Him today!

The Thousand Years

Revelation 20:1-6

¹ *And I saw an angel coming down out of heaven, having the key to the Abyss and holding in his hand a great chain.* ² *He seized the dragon, that ancient serpent, who is the devil, or Satan, and*

bound him for a thousand years. [3] *He threw him into the Abyss, and locked and sealed it over him, to keep him from deceiving the nations anymore until the thousand years were ended. After that, he must be set free for a short time.* [4] *I saw thrones on which were seated those who had been given authority to judge. And I saw the souls of those who had been beheaded because of their testimony for Jesus and because of the word of God. They had not worshiped the beast or his image and had not received his mark on their foreheads or their hands. They came to life and reigned with Christ a thousand years.* [5] *(The rest of the dead did not come to life until the thousand years were ended.) This is the first resurrection.* [6] *Blessed and holy are those who have part in the first resurrection. The second death has no power over them, but they will be priests of God and of Christ and will reign with him for a thousand years.*

* Revelation 20:1-3 → By this point in your journey through the Apocalypse of Jesus Christ, you will have noticed how often John is found marveling at the angels' glory and power. The truth is there are angels more powerful than Satan. These verses inform us that a single angel will descend from heaven to earth, seize Satan, bind him with a great chain, throw him violently into the Abyss, and lock him there for one thousand years (remember that the Abyss is not the eternal lake of fire, Gehenna). This angel's power, however, is like a drop in an ocean when compared to the unimaginable power of our great God and Savior, the Lord Jesus Christ.

During this thousand-year period, which will begin immediately after the seven years of the Tribulation/Great Tribulation and second coming of Jesus, the earth's inhabitants will experience booming growth in both spiritual and natural ways. Satan will be unable to influence the world. All mediums that he uses to corrupt the world and lead people away from God will be purged of his influence. The world's economic and political systems will fall under the theocracy of the Lord's reign. There will be no corruption or lewdness found in media. The global drug syndicates and prostitution rings will be eradicated. Righteousness will reign. He will accomplish that for which all superheroes fight for: justice, peace, and safety for all.

The earth's population will be replenished and multiply tremendously, at an exponential pace that far exceeds any other generation. The reason for this is because there will be no issues of overt sin, evil, or results of sin that currently impact population growth (i.e., murder, abortion, starvation and malnutrition, disease, and death in war). After Christ's thousand-year reign on earth, Satan will be set free from the Abyss for a short while (we'll dive into the reason for this when studying Revelation 20:7-10).

* Revelation 20:4 → Believers in Jesus Christ will not only live eternally with the Lord, but they will also rule and reign with Him over His universal kingdom. Old Testament, New Testament and Tribulation believers (saints) who have been resurrected from the dead will be granted authority with Christ over the kingdoms of the earth for this thousand-year period, a utopian period referred to as the millennial reign of Christ. The level of authority and leadership that Christ will give to his disciples in the new kingdom will be directly related to the level of their faithfulness in serving Him, helping others, and using their talents and gifts for God while they lived on earth prior to the second coming.

The new population on earth during this thousand-year earthly reign of Christ will be comprised of two other groups of people: (1) those who will come to faith in Jesus during the seven-year Tribulation/Great Tribulation period and escape being martyred, surviving until the second coming of Jesus and (2) their offspring.

Isaiah the prophet received from God, almost 800 years before John recorded Revelation, the following prophecy about life during the Millennial reign of Christ:

> "See, I will create new heavens and a new earth. The former things will not be remembered, nor will they come to mind. But be glad and rejoice forever in what I will create, for I will create Jerusalem to be a delight and its people a joy. I will rejoice over Jerusalem and take delight in my people, the sound of weeping and of crying will be heard in it no more. Never again will there be in it an infant who lives but a few days, or an old man who does not live out his years; the one who dies at a hundred will be thought a mere child; the one who fails to reach a hundred will be considered accursed. They will build houses and dwell in them; they will plant vineyards and eat their fruit. No longer will they build houses and others live in them, or plant and others eat. For as the days of a tree, so will be the days of my people; my chosen ones will long enjoy the work of their hands. They will not labor in vain, nor will they bear children doomed to misfortune; for they will be a people blessed by the Lord, they and their descendants with them. Before they call I will answer; while they are still speaking I will hear. The wolf and the lamb will feed together, and the lion will eat straw like the ox, and dust will be the serpent's food. They will neither harm nor destroy on all my holy mountain," says the Lord. [Isaiah 65:17-25].

As a fun and hypothetical exercise, consider the enormous potential size of the earth's population at the end of the one thousand years:

Recall from our hypothetical scenario discussed when examining Revelation 9:13-21 that, if the global population at the start of the Tribulation was approximately 7 billion, that number would be reduced by 55% by the beginning of the Great Tribulation period (second 3.5 years), leaving just over 3 billion. During the second 3.5 years (the Great Tribulation), the majority of humanity will join the kingdom of the Beast (Antichrist) and worship of Satan. Thus, they will not enter the millennial reign of Christ.

Assume out of the four billion people who survive the first 3.5 years of God's judgment (Tribulation), that only 20 percent are Christ-followers and physically survive Satan's and Antichrist's persecution. Then 800 million would enter the millennium. If the number of babies born to these people in the future is the same percentage born today (1.9 percent of total population), the number of babies born during the first year in the millennial kingdom would be 15.2 million (800 million people x .019).

As I typed this paragraph during summer of 2016, the website Worldometers, www.worldometers.info, approximated that 125,380 children would be born that day and 36.6 million would be born for the year. Thus, we see that the 15.2 million born to a reduced population during the first year of the millennial kingdom is more than plausible.

Using a basic compound interest formula, there would be, in our scenario, approximately 119,474,162,106,240,128 (or 199.5 quintillion) people on the earth at the end of the thousand-year reign of Christ on earth. This number *does not* consider the current percentage (.8%) of the earth's population that die on an annual basis today because there will be virtually no one dying in the Millennium Kingdom of Christ.

Does the number above seem outrageous to you? Well, on November 1, 1992, Discover Magazine published an article entitled, *How Many People Can Earth Hold?* The article stated, "Our urge to go forth and multiply could, a century and a half from now, leave earth with more than 694 billion people—some 125 times our current populations."[14] Thus, secular (non-religious) scientists have confirmed that the population explosion scenario I just provided is credible. Remember, the scenario used for illustration purposes does not include a measurable death rate when compared to the birth rate.

* **Revelation 20:5** → Here the "rest of the dead [who] did not come to life until the thousand years were ended" are addressed. These people are all those who have lived and died having never surrendered to the Lordship of Jesus. They will be in Hades for the one thousand-year period, then resurrected to have one-on-one meetings (judgments) with the Lord Himself [to be discussed in the review of Revelation 20:11-15]. Their next and final destination is Gehenna (hell, the eternal lake of fire).

* **Revelation 20:6** → With regard to the phrase "second death", referred to in the last sentence of this verse, I heard a statement years ago that sums up its meaning: All who trust Jesus will die once (physically) and live twice (physically and spiritually); all who reject Jesus will live once (physically) but die twice (physically and spiritually). So, the second death deals specifically with being condemned to eternal punishment in hell (Gehenna, which is the eternal lake of fire).

The Judgment of Satan

Revelation 20:7-10

> [7] *When the thousand years are over, Satan will be released from his prison* [8] *and will go out to deceive the nations in the four corners of the earth—Gog and Magog—to gather them for battle. In number they are like the sand on the seashore.* [9] *They marched across the breadth of the*

earth and surrounded the camp of God's people,
the city he loves. But fire came down from heaven
and devoured them. [10] *And the devil, who deceived*
them, was thrown into the lake of burning sulfur,
where the beast and the false prophet had been
thrown. They will be tormented day and night for
ever and ever.

* **Revelation 20:7-10** → When the thousand-year period comes to a close, Satan will be freed from the Abyss. You may be asking, "Why would Satan be released from this prison?" That's a logical and legitimate question. The Bible has the answer. Let's first set the stage with the information below.

Remember that at the beginning of the Millenial reign of Christ, humans who love Jesus and survive the Tribulation and Great Tribulation periods will enter this thousand-year kingdom. They will have children, who in turn will have offspring – and so on. At the end of this thousand year period, the earth's population will have exploded. However, many born during this time will never have yielded their hearts to Jesus as their personal Lord and Savior. They live good and honorable lives during the thousand-year period and have an outward appearance of obedience to the Lord Jesus and his rule on earth. However, they will not truly love him or earnestly want to serve him. So when Satan is freed at the end of the thousand years, these people will be tempted by him and subsequently follow him. They will fall for Satan's lies just like those who lived before the Millennium - as far back as Adam & Eve to present day.

So back to the question: Why would God allow Satan to be freed from the Abyss to tempt the offspring of the believers who will survive the Great Tribulation? Without question, one of God's purposes in allowing this is to prove, without any shadow of doubt, that the core cause of man's rebellion against Him is neither Satan's influence nor the presence of evil in the world, since there will be neither of these during the Millennial Reign. The rebellion of millions after Satan is released from the Abyss will make it clear once and for all that mankind's sinful nature, inherited from Adam and Eve, is the source of our rebellion.

Why would God take this route? Because countless millions throughout history, and even today, state that if God was truly a loving God, he would make their lives easier - and then they would naturally love, follow, and obey him. Basically, they're saying that if we had a utopian society, where no one suffered and evil influences were wiped away, then people would automatically love others, live right, and honor the Lord. God will prove this to be erroneous thinking. Mankind's sinful nature is opposed to God. He will show that even when mankind lives in a utopian-type world, the sinful heart (focused on what "self" wants) can *and will* reject God. It is not by works that we can redeem ourselves. Even in the best of scenarios, our hearts will betray us when it comes to standing before God on our own merit as righteous and holy. We need a Savior. Christ Jesus is the One and Only Savior as we read in Acts 4:12: "Nor is there salvation in any other, for there is no other name under heaven given among men by which we must be saved."

Chapter 38

A Great White Throne and the Lake of Fire

Revelation 20:11-15

Apocalypse: "The old world passes away, together we shall forge a new one in fire and blood. The future is transformed. 1 am the instrument to purify the world. The evil of humans and mutants must be cut away."

[X-Men The Animated Series: Come the Apocalypse]

As discussed, the majority of Apocalypse's profound state-ments about his plans for the future are derived from pas- sages in the Bible. The one above is no different. Take a look at these verses: Revelation 20:11 and 2 Peter 3:3-13 (which we've already looked at in our discussion of Revelation 16). The evil of humans and demonic spirits that dishonor God and ridicule both his character and creation will one day cease to exist. Jesus is the One who will purify the world. Check out what he said to his early followers:

> Do not suppose that I have come to bring peace to the earth. I did not come to bring peace, but a sword. [Matthew 10:34]

> I have come to bring fire on the earth, and how I wish it were already kindled! [Luke 12:49]

The Judgment of the Dead

Revelation 20:11-15

> [11] *Then I saw a great white throne and him who was seated on it. Earth and sky fled from his presence, and there was no place for them.* [12] *And I saw the dead, great and small, standing before the throne, and books were opened. Another book was opened, which is the book of life. The dead were judged according to what they had done as recorded in the books.* [13] *The sea gave up the dead that were in it, and death and Hades gave up the dead that were in them, and each person was judged according to what he had done.* [14] *Then death and Hades were thrown into the lake of fire. The lake of fire is the second death.* [15] *If anyone's name was not found written in the book of life, he was thrown into the lake of fire.*

   * **Revelation 20:11** → Did you know that Jesus will be seated on the great white throne as the judge of mankind? The Bible makes this truth abundantly clear:

> Therefore since we are God's offspring, we should not think that the divine being is like gold or silver or stone—an image made by human design and skill. In the past God overlooked such ignorance, but now he commands all people everywhere to repent. For he has set a day when he will judge the world with justice by the man he has appointed. He has

given proof of this to everyone by raising him from the dead. [Acts 17:29-31]

For it is not those who hear the law who are righteous in God's sight, but it is those who obey the law who will be declared righteous. (Indeed, when Gentiles, who do not have the law, do by nature things required by the law, they are a law for themselves, even though they do not have the law. They show that the requirements of the law are written on their hearts, their consciences also bearing witness, and their thoughts sometimes accusing them and at other times even defending them.) This will take place on the day when God judges people's secrets through Jesus Christ, as my gospel declares. [Romans 2:13-16]

* **Revelation 20:12** → At the great white throne judgment, all people throughout the annals of time who have not placed their faith in God the Creator and walked in obedience to Him will stand individually before Him. Ushered before the Judge of the universe, they will have to give an account for their lives regarding sin, righteousness, and judgment. This verse tells us that regardless of their status while on earth – whether wealthy or poor, famous or insignificant, giving or miserly – they will be judged without partiality by the only just and holy One.

The reference to books indicates that God will make judgments based on the facts of each person's life. The books will contain more than the recorded words and deeds of each person. They will also contain the inner desires, thoughts, motives, and secret intents of the hearts of all judged. Without the atoning blood of Jesus Christ as the payment for their proven sins against God, they will be convicted as law-breakers and rebels. God's judgment will be fair, clear, and right – with evidence that cannot be refuted.

Friends, think about the surveillance systems of banks, stores, and governments around the world and how they help authorities determine truths about wrongdoing (capturing people on camera who steal, hide, and hurt others). God's surveillance system is everywhere, even in the hearts and minds of every person:

> Nothing in all creation is hidden from God's sight. Everything is uncovered and laid bare before the eyes of him to whom we must give account. [Hebrews 4:13]

*** Revelation 20:13-15** → As previously discussed, Hades (a Greek word translated "hell" in English) is where the souls of all people who are not born again go when they die prior to the Great White Throne Judgment [read Luke 16:19-31]. After the great white throne judgment, people will be cast into hell (Greek word Gehenna) also referred to as the eternal lake of fire. Revelation 20:15 should move people to settle once and for all their own eternal destiny and also to implore others to submit to the love and lordship of Jesus Christ. If you have confessed (acknowledged) your sinful state before God and trusted Jesus Christ as your Savior and Lord, then God expects much from you. You may be the only one in your circle of relationships (family, friends and co-workers) who has ever read the book of Revelation. Therefore, you are now equipped and expected to share with others the realities laid out in it, imploring them to trust Christ Jesus as their Lord and Savior.

If you have not yet surrendered to the Lordship of Jesus Christ, then you have some serious decisions to make. If Jesus is either a liar or lunatic, then you have nothing to be concerned with and everything you have read thus far is hogwash. However, if you believe that Jesus is neither a liar nor a lunatic, the only other option is that He is, indeed, Lord. The decision is now yours to accept or reject his offer of granting you forgiveness of sins and eternal life. Furthermore, it is now your decision to either share or hold back what's been unveiled to you in the book of the Apocalypse of Jesus – as it pertains to your family and friends.

Chapter 39

The New Jerusalem –
Live, Work, Play and Praise

Revelation 21:1-27

Mystiqe: "I am a shape-shifter, an outcast – even among mutants. Trusted by no one. I don't have a life of my own. I just steal little bits from other people's lives. And that's how I survive. So there's your truth son. I didn't want you! Still sad for me?
Nightcrawler: "I will beg God to bestow his grace on me so that I may learn to forgive you. Then I will ask him to bestow his grace on you – so that you might forgive yourself."
Mystique: "I almost got you killed to save my own skin. Why should you or your God care about me?"
Nightcrawler: "As for God, he cares for all of us and wants us to be healed. As for me, you are my mother. I cannot change the pain you have caused me; so I will pray for you.
Mystique: "I don't deserve your…prayers.

[X-Men The Animated Series: Bloodlines]

In the verbal exchange above, Nightcrawler extends forgiveness, grace, and love to his mother. The essence of God's message to the world, as demonstrated through his truth and acts in the Bible, is that he loves all people – though they are wayward and rebellious. He offers His forgiveness and grace to all. Sadly, however, many still refuse that love.

The New Jerusalem

Revelation 21:1-4

> [1] *Then I saw a new heaven and a new earth, for the first heaven and the first earth had passed away, and there was no longer any sea.* [2] *I saw the Holy City, the new Jerusalem, coming down out of heaven from God, prepared as a bride beautifully dressed for her husband.* [3] *And I heard a loud voice from the throne saying, "Now the dwelling of God is with men, and he will live with them. They will be his people, and God himself will be with them and be their God.* [4] *He will wipe every tear from their eyes. There will be no more death or mourning or crying or pain, for the old order of things has passed away."*

* **Revelation 21:1** → In this verse, John states that after the great white throne judgment, God will bring about a new heaven and new earth.

The apostle Peter relayed prophetic truth regarding the passing away of the current heavens (atmosphere and outer space) and earth:

> ...the present heavens and earth are reserved for fire, being kept for the day of judgment and destruction of the ungodly...The heavens will disappear with a roar; the elements will be destroyed by fire, and the earth and everything done in it will be laid bare. [II Peter 3:3-18]

Jesus talked about this reality as well.

> For truly I tell you, until heaven and earth disappear, not the smallest letter, not the least stroke of a pen, will by any means disappear from the Law until everything is accomplished. [Matthew 5:18]

> Heaven and earth will pass away, but my words will never pass away. [Mark 13:31]

PAUSE...

Friends, this is not a made-up story. This is real and it will happen. If not, then Jesus is a liar and the Bible is an assembly of concocted myths and lies, neither worth reading nor suitable for aligning one's life. God has drawn a line in the sands of time and eternity and each person will have to decide on which side of this line they will stand or fall. There is, frankly, no middle ground. Have you made the firmest and wisest decision you can ever make in life? Have you surrendered to the lordship and love of the Lord Jesus Christ?

* Revelation 21:2-4 → John sees the Holy City that has come from heaven, the New Jerusalem, descending from heaven to the new earth. Jesus is preparing this mind-blowing dwelling place for all those who trust Him. Before his crucifixion, Jesus made the following statement, applicable to all of his followers:

> Do not let your hearts be troubled. You trust in God; trust also in me. In my Father's house are many rooms; if it were not so, I would have told you. I am going there to prepare a place for you. And if I go and prepare a place for you, I will come back and take you to be with me that you may also be where I am. [John 14:1-3]

All who place their trust in the Lord Jesus will one day dwell with God and the Lamb (Jesus), in resurrected and eternal bodies. With the New Jerusalem as their home, those redeemed by the blood of Christ will have all of eternity to enjoy and explore the creation of the new heavens and earth. What God has planned is beyond what mankind can comprehend:

> ...No eye has seen, no ear has heard, no mind has conceived what God has prepared for those who love him. [I Corinthians 2:9]

The Enthroned One Speaks

Revelation 21:5-8

> *[5] He who was seated on the throne said, "I am making everything new!" Then he said, "Write this down, for these words are trustworthy and true." [6] He said to me: "It is done. I am the Alpha and the Omega, the Beginning and the End. To him who is thirsty I will give to drink without cost from the spring of the water of life. [7] He who overcomes will inherit all this, and I will be his God and he will be my son. [8] But the cowardly, the unbelieving, the vile, the murderers, the sexually immoral, those who practice magic arts, the idolaters and all liars—their place will be in the fiery lake of burning sulfur. This is the second death."*

* **Revelation 21:5** → Jesus is enthroned as King of kings and Lord of lords. He told the first twelve disciples that he was going to make new everything in God's creation:

> I tell you the truth, at the renewal of all things, when the Son of Man sits on his glorious throne, you who have followed me will also sit on twelve thrones, judging the twelve tribes of Israel. And everyone who has left houses or brother or sisters or father or mother or children or fields for my sake will receive a hundred times as much and will inherit eternal life. [Matthew 19:28-29]

* **Revelation 21:6-7** → More proof that the Eternal One sitting on the throne is Jesus, as evidenced by his title 'Alpha and Omega (refer to Revelation 1:4-8) as well as his desire and ability to give living water (eternal life) to all who come to him:

> Jesus answered, "Everyone who drinks this water will be thirsty again, but whoever drinks the water I give them will never thirst. Indeed, the water I give them will become in them a spring of water welling up to eternal life." [John 4:13-14]

* **Revelation 21:8** → Note that the first descriptor that Jesus uses to characterize the group of people listed in verse eight is "the cowardly". Sadly, many let the thoughts and opinions of others prevent them from living courageous lives for the Lord. Their desire to be accepted by others squeezes out their desire to believe in him. Failure to believe in Him leads people into various sinful activities and habits, such as those listed in this verse. Don't let this characterization be the reality of your life and haunt you for eternity, which will include weeping and gnashing of teeth. Like superheroes in the comics and movies, dare to be courageous, not cowardly.

Superheroes risk their lives daily to combat villains and bring to justice people who match the characterization of those listed in Revelation 21:8, people who are vile, murderers, sexually perverse, who practice dark and secretive methods to do evil, and who compromise truth as liars. Millions of people applaud fictional superheroes for using the law and righteous standards for both judging and punishing evildoers. But many of these same people reject the real and almighty God of the universe for upholding the same standards of righteousness. Sadly, their punishment will be justified and certain.

Details of the Heavenly City

Revelation 21:9-27

> [9] *One of the seven angels who had the seven bowls full of the seven last plagues came and said to me, "Come, I will show you the bride, the wife of the Lamb."* [10] *And he carried me away in the Spirit to a mountain great and high, and showed me the Holy City, Jerusalem, coming down out of heaven from God.* [11] *It shone with the glory of God, and its brilliance was like that of a very precious jewel, like a jasper, clear as crystal.* [12] *It had a great, high wall with twelve gates, and with twelve angels at the gates. On the gates were written the names of the twelve tribes of Israel.* [13] *There were three gates on the east, three on the north, three on the south and three on the west.* [14] *The wall of the city had twelve foundations, and on them were the names of the twelve apostles of the Lamb.* [15] *The angel who talked with me had a measuring rod of gold to measure the city, its gates and its walls.* [16] *The city was laid out like a square, as long as it was wide. He measured the city with the rod and found it to be 12,000 stadia in length, and*

as wide and high as it is long. [17] *He measured its wall and it was 144 cubits thick, by man's measurement, which the angel was using.* [18] *The wall was made of jasper, and the city of pure gold, as pure as glass.* [19] *The foundations of the city walls were decorated with every kind of precious stone. The first foundation was jasper, the second sapphire, the third chalcedony, the fourth emerald,* [20] *the fifth sardonyx, the sixth carnelian, the seventh chrysolite, the eighth beryl, the ninth topaz, the tenth chrysoprase, the eleventh jacinth, and the twelfth amethyst.* [21] *The twelve gates were twelve pearls, each gate made of a single pearl. The great street of the city was of pure gold, like transparent glass.* [22] *I did not see a temple in the city, because the Lord God Almighty and the Lamb are its temple.* [23] *The city does not need the sun or the moon to shine on it, for the glory of God gives it light, and the Lamb is its lamp.* [24] *The nations will walk by its light, and the kings of the earth will bring their splendor into it.* [25] *On no day will its gates ever be shut, for there will be no night there.* [26] *The glory and honor of the nations will be brought into it.* [27] *Nothing impure will ever enter it, nor will anyone who does what is shameful or deceitful, but only those whose names are written in the Lamb's book of life.*

* **Revelation 21:9-26** → The New Jerusalem, the Holy City, will be the home of all Christians (also called God's holy people, the bride of Christ, and saints) who trusted Christ as Savior and Lord. It will be massive beyond our comprehension. 12,000 stadia is equivalent to 1,380 miles. Thus, this cube-like city will be 1,380 miles long, 1,380 miles wide, and 1,380 miles high.

Did you get that? Okay, let's take a close-up look at the mind-blowing dimensions of the Holy City to come. The United States is approximately 3,000 miles wide, from east coast to west coast. The New Jerusalem will be about half this distance in width, as well as being the same distance in both its length and height. Imagine a 5-Star hotel with a first floor that is 1,300 miles wide and 1,300 miles long. The equivalent, in square feet would be 47,114,496,000,000 square feet (1,300 miles x 5280 feet/mile x 1,300 miles x 5,280 feet/mile). And this is just the first floor!! If there were 5,000 sq ft condos on just the first floor, this is enough space for 9.4 billion condos (again, on just the first floor).

The New Jerusalem's height will be 6,864,000 feet high (1,300 miles x 5,280 feet/mile). For perspective, the distance from the earth to the moon is approximately 1,261,154,400 feet (238,855 miles). So don't think that the New Jerusalem will be reaching into far outer space. It's a "mere" .5% the distance from the earth to the moon. However, the height of the New Jerusalem blows away the tallest man-made buildings in the world, such as the 2,722 ft high Burj Khalifa in Dubai or Saudi Arabia's 3,280 ft high Jeddah Tower (scheduled for completion in 2020). The New Jerusalem's total size (width x length x height) will be a staggering 16,169,695,027,200,000,000 cubic feet. As you read in verses 9-26, the New Jerusalem is not only massive, it is also stunning – adorned with creation's most precious stones and resources – as well as with things never seen nor imagined.

  * **Revelation 21:27** → Many people say that they want to go to heaven when they die. God has given us the criteria and standards for entering: *perfection*. While impure sinners don't meet that qualification, Jesus does. He came to earth and willingly laid his life down as a ransom for our lives, granting us His righteousness and taking our unrighteousness upon Himself. Have you surrendered yet to the One who loves you and gave His life for you? An eternal future awaits us all. It is our decision to either accept or reject the Lord Jesus Christ.

Chapter 40

Jesus' Last Words – Listen Well

Revelation 22:1-21

Apocalypse: "From the ashes of this world, I will build a better one. "

[X-Men The Animated Series: Come the Apocalypse]

"Ashes to ashes, dust to dust" is a phrase commonly found in eulogies. Just as every book has a last chapter and movies have closing scenes, our lives too will have a definite ending. How will your life's story end with regard to where your soul will go the moment you die? The ultimate landing place for all of us regarding our eternal destinies will be either heaven or hell. Jesus gave his life that you might be heaven-bound. Regardless of who accepts or rejects him, His plans will come to fruition. His purpose is not to merely build a better world. No, he will bring about that which only fits his nature – perfection with no sin ever again.

The River of Life

Revelation 22:1-6

¹ *Then the angel showed me the river of the water of life, as clear as crystal, flowing from the throne of God and of the Lamb* ² *down the middle of the*

great street of the city. On each side of the river stood the tree of life, bearing twelve crops of fruit, yielding its fruit every month. And the leaves of the tree are for the healing of the nations. ³ No longer will there be any curse. The throne of God and of the Lamb will be in the city, and his servants will serve him. ⁴ They will see his face, and his name will be on their foreheads. ⁵ There will be no more night. They will not need the light of a lamp or the light of the sun, for the Lord God will give them light. And they will reign for ever and ever. ⁶ The angel said to me, "These words are trustworthy and true. The Lord, the God of the spirits of the prophets, sent his angel to show his servants the things that must soon take place."

* Revelation 22:1-6 → This section of Scripture is summarized by the angel's words in verse six, "...These words are trustworthy and true. The Lord, the God of the spirits of the prophets, sent his angel (messenger) to show his servants the things that must soon take place." Do you believe what you have read thus far? Whether you do or don't will not change the truth. FACT: Neither active rebellion nor passive indifference will prevent the realities of the future from occurring. Therefore, live wisely!

> Just as people are destined to die once, and after that to face judgment, so Christ was sacrificed once to take away the sins of many; and he will appear a second time, not to bear sin, but to bring salvation to those who are waiting for him. [Hebrews 9:27-28]

Jesus Is Coming

Revelation 22:7-11

[7] *"Behold, I am coming soon! Blessed is he who keeps the words of the prophecy in this book."* [8] *I, John, am the one who heard and saw these things. And when I had heard and seen them, I fell down to worship at the feet of the angel who had been showing them to me.* [9] *But he said to me, "Do not do it! I am a fellow servant with you and with your brothers the prophets and of all who keep the words of this book. Worship God!"* [10] *Then he told me, "Do not seal up the words of the prophecy of this book, because the time is near.* [11] *Let him who does wrong continue to do wrong; let him who is vile continue to be vile; let him who does right continue to do right; and let him who is holy continue to be holy."*

* **Revelation 22:7** → This verse has two guaranteed promises. First, Jesus is coming again. Second, those who take to heart (hear *and* act) what God has taught through the Revelation of Jesus Christ will be blessed – both in this temporary life and, more importantly, in the eternal one to come.

* **Revelation 22:8-11** → Remember the stern rebuke of Jesus to the church of Laodiceans in Revelation 3:14-16:

> These are the words of the Amen, the faithful and true witness, the ruler of God's creation. I know your deeds, that you are neither cold nor hot. I wish you were either one or the other! So, because you are lukewarm – neither hot nor cold – I am about to spit you out of my mouth.

Keeping these words in mind will give deeper meaning to Revelation 22:8-11. Jesus demands a decision from each person on whether or not they deem Him worthy to be followed. What choice have you made? If you were to die today, what would be your eternal destiny? Tomorrow is not promised. What is preventing you from surrendering to the love and Lordship of Jesus? Submit to him and begin living as his disciple. Great will be your reward.

The Beckoning and the Warning

Revelation 22:12-21

[12] *"Behold, I am coming soon! My reward is with me, and I will give to everyone according to what he has done.* [13] *I am the Alpha and the Omega, the First and the Last, the Beginning and the End.* [14] *"Blessed are those who wash their robes, that they may have the right to the tree of life and may go through the gates into the city.* [15] *Outside are the dogs, those who practice magic arts, the sexually immoral, the murderers, the idolaters and everyone who loves and practices falsehood.* [16] *"I, Jesus, have sent my angel to give you this testimony for the churches. I am the Root and the Offspring of David, and the bright Morning Star."* [17] *The Spirit and the bride say, "Come!" And let him who hears say, "Come!" Whoever is thirsty, let him come; and whoever wishes, let him take the free gift of the water of life.* [18] *I warn everyone who hears the words of the prophecy of this book: If anyone adds anything to them, God will add to him the plagues described in this book.* [19]*

And if anyone takes words away from this book of prophecy, God will take away from him his share in the tree of life and in the holy city, which are described in this book. [20] *He who testifies to these things says, "Yes, I am coming soon." Amen. Come, Lord Jesus.* [21] *The grace of the Lord Jesus be with God's people. Amen.*

* **Revelation 22:12-21** → *"Coming Soon!"* are the words that millions long for when they hear about or see a trailer for the latest superhero movie. Well, the "book-end" verses of this section of Scripture, Revelation 22:12 and 22:20, have the emphatic words of Jesus stating, "...I am coming soon" – which equate to the words, "I am inevitable". In Revelation 22:18 and 22:19, Jesus Himself gives all mankind a warning regarding adding to or taking away from the words of the prophetic book's purpose/message.

Chapter 41

So Now That You Know...(Decide Well)

News Anchor: "It seems only by the grace of God that the ominous destruction seen from one end of the globe to the other... [fades to the next voice]
United States Federal Agent: "I think our prayers were answered. Thank you Mr. President."

[X-Men: Apocalypse]

Just after Apocalypse's defeat in the movie *X-Men: Apocalypse*, media outlets across the world began sharing the news of how the earth and its inhabitants had been spared from global destruction. More specifically, the journalists' accredited the miraculous deliverance to God, speaking of answered prayers and His grace. It's pretty cool that the writers, directors, and producers of *X-Men: Apocalypse* included this overt acknowledgement of mankind's true dependency on God when catastrophes hit.

There are two distinct ways in which God's grace, defined as His unmerited favor, has been shed on mankind. One expression of his general grace extended to mankind – who for the most part do not acknowledge him in any way on a daily basis – is associated with all that he provides people for general living in the world. For example, everyone alive today is a recipient of God's grace because thousands of others across the globe, who were alive on yesterday, did not live to see today. Every person who drank water today was a grantee of God's grace because a third of the world's population is suffering from a shortage of water. Every person who ate food today should thank God for his goodness extended to him or her. Why? Because, by his grace, they are not part of the eleven percent of the world's population who don't have enough to eat on a daily basis.

The second expression of God's grace pertains specifically to the spiritual realm. His offer to forgive sins and reconcile mankind to Himself was accomplished through the birth, life, crucifixion, and resurrection of the Lord Jesus Christ. All who believe that Jesus is who claims to be and submits to His lordship will be recipients of God's saving grace, being forgiven as transgressors of His laws and pardoned from the penalty of sin.

When it comes to all that has been shared in this book, one must make life-altering choices. Death will not wait for anyone. It most often comes at an unexpected hour. The stark reality is that death is the gateway to our eternal destiny. Our feelings and emotions are indeed important, but the volition (the power to make our own choices or decisions) is what matters most as we move forward in life towards eternity. Just as the training means nothing without the will to act, so is the accumulation of knowledge about God without the resolve to bow in obedience to his sovereignty.

All people will make a decision to either accept or reject God's truths. Indecision and passivity are, in fact, firm decisions of rejection. While the jurors of logic, facts, and truth beckon all to surrender to the God, they will also be condemning witnesses against all who choose to reject God's forgiving grace. God is powerful enough to force us to believe in him, but that type of belief would not be associated with volitional love and willful obedience. No, the choice is ours to either accept or reject his love and forgiveness.

So, as is the case in every area of life in which you must make crucial decisions, be very careful to proceed with wisdom when it comes to your eternal destiny. It is my hope that you have been enlightened by the truth presented in this book and brought to a place of clear decision-making regarding your understanding of biblical truth. God's apocalypse is not one to be feared or rejected. Rather, what He has revealed about the unstoppable future return of the Lord Jesus Christ should be embraced, accepted, and treasured. Are you ready to begin devoting yourself to the truths and ideals set forth by God, revealed in the book of Revelation? Are you ready to allow your heart, mind, and life be transformed into something entirely new? The Hero of all heroes, the Lord Jesus Christ, will one day return to the earth. He is able to rescue you and fulfill all of your hopes and dreams – for both this temporal life and the eternal one to come. As God promises us in his word [II Corinthians 5:17:

> Therefore, if anyone is in Christ, he is a new creation; old things have passed away; behold, all things have become new.

Comic Superhero Index

Footnotes

1 Callahan, Timothy (September 28, 2009). "When Words Collide". Comic Book Resources.

2 Polycarp.net

3 http://www.answersintheendtimes.com/Sunday-School-Lessons/Pt-19-The-Church-at-Sardis

4 http://www.fishingtheabyss.com/archives/29

5 Heller, Eva (2009). Psychologie de la couleur – Effets et symboliques. Pyramyd (French translation). ISBN 978-2-35017-156-2; pp. 87-104.

6 Heller, Eva (2009). Psychologie de la couleur – Effets et symboliques. Pyramyd (French translation). ISBN 978-2-35017-156-2; pp. 98.

7 "UN Press Release: World population projected to reach 9.6 billion by 2050 with most growth in developing regions, especially Africa" (PDF). United Nations Department of Economic and Social Affairs. June 13, 2013. Retrieved March 16, 2015.

8 Science News, Earth Has Four Corners, Magazine issue: Vol. 87 #25, June 19, 1965; https://www.sciencenews.org/archive/earth-hasfour-corners?mode=magazine&context=1385.

9 http://www.thepeopleoftruth.com/BibleGuys/feb99/ScienceandtheBible.html

10 http://nabataea.net/siq.html, Petra – Capital City of Nabataea.[chap12:14]

11 Archaeology of Palestine, Art of Excavating a Palestinian Mound, William Foxwell Albright, 1960, p. 16 [chap 16:15]

12 https://www.weather.gov/media/abr/vivian/073010RecordHail VivianSD.pdf, "South Dakota Storm Produces Record Hailstone", National Oceanic and Atmospheric Administration, Press Release, July 30, 2010. [chap16:21]

13 http://www.bibleinterp.com/articles/2001/cli268001.shtml, The Battles of Armageddon: Megiddo and the Jezreel Valley from the Bronze Age to the Nuclear Age, Eric Cline, Assistant Professor of Archaeology and Ancient History, Department of Classical and Semitic Languages and Literatures, The George Washington University 2001. [chap 19:17,18]

14 http://discovermagazine.com/1992/nov/howmanypeoplecan152, How Many People Can Earth Hold?, By Joel E. Cohen, Sunday, November 01, 1992 [chap 20:4]

www.ingramcontent.com/pod-product-compliance
Lightning Source LLC
Chambersburg PA
CBHW052032090426
42739CB00010B/1870